everything yearned for

everything yearned for

MANHAE'S POEMS OF LOVE AND LONGING

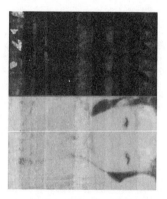

A TRANSLATION OF MANHAE'S

THE SILENCE OF EVERYTHING YEARNED FOR

Translated and Introduced by Francisca Cho

foreword by David R. McCann

Wisdom Publications
199 Elm Street
Somerville, MA 02144 USA
www.wisdompubs.org

Library of Congress Cataloging-in-Publication Data
Cho, Francisca.
  Everything yearned for : Manhae's poems of love and longing / a translation
of Manhae's the silence of everything yearned for, translated and introduced
by Francisca Cho.
      p. cm.
  Includes bibliographical references and index.
  ISBN 0-86171-489-X (hardcover : alk. paper)
  1. Han, Yong-un, 1879–1944—Criticism and interpretation. 2. Han, Yong-un,
1879–1944—Translations into English. I. Han, Yong-un, 1879–1944. II. Title.

PL991.26.Y6A23 2004
895.7'13—dc22

                                        2004020460

First Edition
09 08 07 06 05
5   4   3   2   1

Poems from *Columbia Anthology of Traditional Korean Poetry*, edited by David R.
McCann, © 2004, Columbia University Press. Reprinted with the permission of the
publisher.

Radbindranath Tagore poems reprinted by permission of The Sahitya Akademi.

Cover design and imagery by Elizabeth Lawrence. A special thank you to
  Kim Lawrence for posing for the photograph.
Interior design by Gopa&Ted2, Inc. Set in Dante MT 11/16.

Printed in Canada.

Table of Contents

Index of Poem Titles

Foreword

The challenges confronting anyone wishing to translate Manhae's poetry are daunting. He is very highly regarded in Korea, both as a poet and Buddhist leader, as well as for his active involvement in the Korean national independence movement during the Japanese colonial occupation. Each year, an annual symposium on his life's work, his poetry, and his Buddhist thought and writing is held in Korea, formerly at Paekdam Temple, and more recently at a new study center, the Manhae Village, constructed in his honor and memory. A major Korean and international award ceremony is held annually in his honor, with awards for Buddhist practice, arts and sciences, literature, and world peace. He is truly an iconic figure.

Manhae left only one published collection of poems, the book we have now in Francisca Cho's remarkable translation. Beyond the imposing figure of Manhae himself, the poems present their own formidable challenges. First, the title of the book and the title poem: *Nim ŭi ch'immuk. Ch'immuk* is not the difficulty: "silence." But the word *nim* is itself a formidable challenge, a microcosm of Manhae himself. It has been translated here as "love," or "the lover," or "the beloved"—and even once, in a sort of formal gesture, left untranslated. Francisca Cho explores the various options, including the range of meanings associated with the word: "*nim* can signify not only a 'lover' in the romantic and erotic sense but also anyone or anything that is held in loving esteem—one's political sovereign, parent, teacher; one's country, humanity, God." How to decide? She chooses to take the definition from Manhae's own preface to the poems, in which he defines *nim* as "not only a human lover but everything yearned for." "That's it exactly!" one wants to shout. The Gordian knot is cut with that one brilliant stroke.

The second and even more daunting question is what to make of Manhae's poems, and in particular, the long rhythmical lines that seem to sweep forward with an almost Biblical cadence in some places, while in others breaking apart into brief, almost conversational phrases. Manhae was not writing poetry like anyone else in Korea at the time. There had been some translations of poets such as Mallarmé, Verlaine, Yeats and poets like Sowŏl, Kim Chôngsik, who adapted traditional Korean folksong forms and figures; but the long, extending line of Manhae's poems, and their mix of the philosophical, mystical, religious, and sensual were uniquely distinctive.

Cho pays high accord to three previous translations, then observes of her own only that she has "aimed for a translation that is faithful both in content and style." She has indeed accomplished both. Manhae did not falter over his lines, and neither does this translator. As I first read through the poems, watching out for infelicities (as one does), I found only a steady, sure control of line and line break, the truest and deepest form of fidelity to Manhae's confident original.

Finally, a word of appreciation for the detailed notes on the poems, and the excellent account of Manhae, his life and his religious thought. One or the other of these can be found in a variety of Korean materials, but nowhere exists a more balanced and clear account. So in this book we find Manhae, his life, work, and thought, in addition to the splendid translations of his poems, for all of which I for one wish simply to thank Francisca Cho. She has provided the definitive English language translation of Manhae's remarkable poems. For readers who will come to this book by a variety of pathways, let me add only: a wonderful voyage awaits you.

David R. McCann

DAVID R. McCann, *recipient of the the Manhae Prize for Arts and Sciences in 2004, is the Korea Foundation Professor of Korean Literature and Director of the Korea Institute at Harvard University.*

Translator's Preface

MANHAE (1879–1944) was a Korean Buddhist monk and a cultural hero who fought for the survival of Korean Buddhism in an age of abrupt modernization and colonial domination. He worked for the educational and institutional reform of Buddhist monasticism and translated Buddhist teachings in a way that was accessible and relevant to ordinary people. His dominant role in the creation of the March 1, 1919, Declaration of Independence from Japanese colonial rule, which earned him a significant place in modern Korean history, indicates the degree to which Manhae's Buddhism was socially engaged. The underlying purpose of his political as well as his religious activities was to aid in the liberation of all beings.

The same can be said of Manhae in his capacity as a poet, which is emerging as his most enduring persona. Presently, Manhae is best remembered for the collection of poetry presented here, *Nim ŭi ch'immuk*, or "The Silence of Everything Yearned For." This volume of poetry presents itself as love poems, but its multilayered senses have spurred readers to a number of allegorical insights as well. While some poems are exquisitely pure in sentiment, others are quite complex, suggesting an array of poetic voices and referents. Some poems are written in a man's voice, others in a woman's, for example. In using the female voice, Manhae employs a traditional poetic practice that abstracts from his personal experiences, but which nevertheless allows for a most direct and ardent form of expression—that of a woman longing for her lover.

The question of how to read and interpret Silence has been the subject of scholarly and cultural debate ever since its publication in 1926. Some of the poems exhibit a clear historical and national consciousness, lending support to the Korean habit of assuming that Manhae's "beloved" is none other than his country of Korea, then lost to Japanese rule. Others have chosen to see in the poems an implicit reference to Buddhist enlightenment as the object of desire. Still others speculate on the possibility of a woman in Manhae's life during the time of composition.

In the essay at the end of this volume, I discuss the historical context of Manhae's poetry and give an account of his life. The primary objective of this translation, however, is to offer the reader an intrinsically enjoyable literary experience—a goal that I believe is faithful to Manhae's intentions. For all of his social and political commitments, Manhae's Buddhist sensibility emphasizes what is immediately present to the senses. The language, imagery, and sensuous texture of his poetry are their own reward, apart from any greater meanings that they may signify.

The spectrum of Manhae's poetic styles is broad. He wrote contemplative nature poetry, dark and tortured symbolic poetry, sensual poems of love and longing, and overtly patriotic addresses. The poems vary significantly in length and in tone. One distinguishing feature of Manhae is his long, prose-style sentences. In the original Korean, they flow in their own internal rhythm; in translation, they create visually awkward, runover sentences that I have broken into separate lines. On occasion I have grouped some lines into independent stanzas to give balance to the text. Otherwise, the structural arrangement of the poems is Manhae's own.

The accepted conceit that Manhae wrote all eighty-eight poems in the course of a single night has inspired scholars to discern a clear narrative scheme in the progression of the anthology. While this is an interesting exercise, it entails rather subjective readings and perhaps also overstates the case for the work's seamlessness. While the collection is meant to be read as all of a piece, each poem can be enjoyed independently. In the notes on the Poems that follow the translation, I indicate some dominant themes and practices. A major leitmotif is departure and reunion, which is worked into the first and last poems to form a loose narrative framing, as well as forming a dominant theme of the entire work.

Manhae's conversation with the Indian poet and Nobel laureate Rabindranath Tagore (1861–1941) is another significant thread woven throughout the anthology, and it is noteworthy for its literary-critical perspective as well as for its historical significance. Some poems reflect a legacy of imagery, conceit, or practice within East Asia that is useful to bring to light, and which demonstrates the continuity of Manhae's poetic practices with the past. A number of poems make specific cultural or historical references that beg for clarification. In other cases, the connotations of certain words or phrases lost in translation call for a note. Every so often I suggest an interpretive option for a poem that is particularly dense in symbolism or complex in sentiment. My aim throughout is to enhance the reader's encounter with Silence rather than to bury the work in scholarly commentary.

It is my hope that this volume will engage an English-speaking audience with the same intensity that Manhae has held his countrymen. The power of longing is the source of religion and art alike. Manhae uses both to speak to us across national, linguistic, and historical distances with brilliance and heart.

Francisca Cho

Translator's Acknowledgments

I would like to thank the generosity of Thomas McKenna and the McKenna Fund in sponsoring the publication of this book. I have immensely benefited, as well, from countless conversations with my mother, Angela, and my husband, Richard. These conversations have inspired my sense of Manhae and my capacity to render him into words.

Publisher's Acknowledgments

Publication of this book has been supported by the Sunshik Min Endowment for the Advancement of Korean Literature, Korea Institute, Harvard University.

The Silence of Everything Yearned For

Preface: Idle Words

"*Nim*" is not only a human lover but everything yearned for.
All beings are *nim* for the Buddha, and philosophy is the *nim* of Kant.
The spring rain is *nim* for the rose, and Italy is the *nim* of Mazzini.
Nim is what I love, but it also loves me.

If romantic love is freedom, then so is my *nim*.
But aren't you attached to the lofty name of freedom?
Don't you also have a *nim*? If so, it's only your shadow.

I write these poems for the young lambs wandering lost
   on the road home from the darkening plains.

1 : *My Lover's Silence*

My love is gone.
Ah, the one I love is gone.
Crossing the narrow path to the maple grove
   that shatters the mountain green, she tore away from me.
Promises, like bright gold blossoms,
turned into ash scattered by gentle wind.
The memory of a sharp first kiss reversed my destiny and then,
retreating, faded away to nothing.
I was deafened by her scented voice;
blinded by her flowerlike face.
Love is a human thing—when meeting I already feared parting,
and still with separation, my heart burst with fresh sorrow.

But to turn parting into useless tears destroys love,
and so I turned the strength of sadness into new hope.
Just as meeting creates worry of parting,
parting creates hope of meeting again.

My love is gone, but I didn't send her away.
My common song of love wraps itself around my lover's silence.

2 : *Parting Creates Beauty*

Parting creates beauty.
The beauty of parting is not in the fragile gold of morning,
in the seamless silk of night,
in deathless immortality,
or the undying blue of heaven.
My love, without parting I wouldn't live again in laughter
    after dying in tears.

Ah, parting.
Beauty creates parting.

3 : *I Don't Know*

Whose footfall is the Paulownia leaf rippling through the still air?

Whose face is the blue sky peeping through the dark clouds
    driven by the zephyr at the rainy season's end?

Whose breath is the unknown fragrance flowing
    through the green moss
in the deep, flowerless woods and brushing the quiet sky
    above the old pagoda?

Whose song is the delicately flowing stream of unknown source
    splashing against the stones?

Whose poetry is the glow that adorns the setting sun,
    with its jadelike hands caressing the endless sky
and its lotuslike heels that cross
    over the boundless ocean?

After burning, embers become fuel again.
Whose faint lamp is my heart, burning for reason unknown
    through the night?

4 : *I Want to Forget*

Others think about their love
but I try to forget mine.
The more I try to forget, the more I remember.

Remembering, I tried to forget,
but if I forget then I remember,
and if I remember, I can't forget.

Shall I try to stop forgetting and remembering?
Shall I try to throw both away?
Neither will work.
What can I do when my love fills every thought?

It's not impossible to forget
in a case of deliberate forgetting.
But that means sleeping or dying,
and because of love I can do neither.

Greater than the remembering that can't be forgotten
is the difficulty of trying to forget.

5 : *Don't Go*

Those aren't love's wings that wrap themselves around the dear child,
snuggling in his mother's breast with pursed lips
   in the expectation of sweetness;
it's the flag of the enemy.
That's not the light of compassion from Buddha's brow;
It's the flash from a demon's eyes.
That's not the goddess of love who binds body and mind,
and tosses herself into love's ocean, caring nothing
   for crowns, glory, or death;
It's the smile of the knife.
My love, you thirst for satisfaction.
Turn around—don't go to that place. I hate it.

The earth's music falls asleep in the Rose of Sharon's shadow.
The dream of prosperity dives deep into the black ocean.
The frightening silence imparts the knife-sharp sermons
   of the whispering universe.
My love, you want to get drunk on the bloom of new life.
Turn around—don't go to that place. I hate it.

Where is the lovely girl who takes the angel-blessed children,
places her own life in them and offers them on love's altar?
Where is the strange lily that offers its sweet and clear perfume
to one honeybee and denies it to the other?
Where is the firefly that buries itself in death's green mountain
and cuts the night in two with its flowing light?
My love, you are ready to die for your passion.
Turn back—don't go to that place. I hate it.

In that land, there is no sky.
In that land, shadowless people war.
In that land, the measureless rhythm of great time
   and the key to creation stops.
My love, you claim that death is fragrant.
Turn back—don't go to that place. I hate it.

6 : *Lonely Night*

No moon in the sky, no breeze on the ground,
no sound of people—and I, empty of mind.

Is the universe death?
Is life sleep?

The golden thread of love's memory attaches to my brow at one end;
to a little star at the other; and gently, gently disappears.
One hand grasps a golden sword, the other plucks celestial flowers,
and the queen of illusion also vanishes.
Who knew that love's golden thread and illusion's queen
would clasp hands, and, in tears, die for each other?

Is the universe death?
Is life tears?

If life is tears,
is death love?

7 ⋮ *My Path*

So many paths in this world—
in the mountain, paths of stone;
in the ocean, waterways;
in the sky, paths of moon and stars.

Along the river, the fisherman makes footprints in the sand.
In the field, the girl picking greens tramples sweet grass.
The evil one travels the way of wrongdoing.
The righteous one walks the blade's edge.
The setting sun treads the reddening sky.
Morning's pure dew glides down flower buds.

As for me, I have two possible paths in this world:
one is the path of your embrace;
the other is death's.
Other paths are worse than dying.

Who lays down my path?
In this world, only you can.
If you have laid down my path,
why that of death as well?

8 ∶ *Waking from a Dream*

If it's you, you would love me,
but is it love to come to my door every night then go,
   leaving only the sound of footsteps?
My footsteps have never been outside your door.
Maybe only you can love?
If your footsteps hadn't awakened me
I would be riding a cloud seeking you.

9 : *The Artist*

I'm a clumsy painter.
Sleepless, my finger traced your nose, your lips,
  even your dimple, on my breast.
Then, I drew the slight smile that hovers around your eyes,
but I erased it a hundred times over.

I'm an amateur singer.
The neighbors gone and the insects quiet, I wanted to sing the song
  you taught me,
but I felt shy seeing the dozing cat.
So I softly joined the chorus of the breeze that fluttered
  against the paper door.

I don't have the makings of a lyric poet.
I don't want to write about "joy" or "sorrow" or "love."
I want to capture exactly your face, your voice, your walk.
I'll write about your house, your bed, and even the pebbles
  in your flower garden.

10 : *Parting*

People are weak, fragile, deceitful.
In this world, parting from real love is not possible.
What parting is there from my lover, who trades love for death?
Parting tears are false flowers, gilded drops of gold.

Where is the parting kiss cut from a knife?
Where is the parting wine brewed from the bloom of life?
Where is the parting ring made from the ruby of blood?
Parting tears are jewels of curses, deceit's crystals.

Parting in love is the opposite of parting;
so there is a greater love in parting.
If not a direct love, then an implied one.
For I love myself more than my departed lover.
If I loved her more than myself, parting would disappear
until moss covers the wheel of time that turns eternity.

No, no. Love is more than "truth"; parting is greater than death.
If death is a drop of cold dew, parting is a deluge of flowers.
If death is a bright star, parting is the glorious sun.
To love someone more than life—you can't die because of this love.

Living in fear for the sake of love is a greater sacrifice than death.
Parting is the price of living for love's sake,
   because you grieve for a lover's death more than for parting itself.
Love isn't only in the candle's red flame or the fresh wine,
it's in the formlessness that mirrors each others' minds
   through the distance.

A lover isn't forgotten in death, she's remembered in parting.
A lover isn't smiled upon in death, she's cried for in parting.
The regret of parting isn't repaid by the comfort of death;
sadness is endured for the lover's sake.
Love can't bear dying, and nothing is greater than love that bears parting.

Real love has no place.
It's not just the embrace of a lover, it's the love of separation.
Real love has no time.
Parting is in body, but love does not end.

For the love of one's lover, death offers a knife; parting offers a flower.
Tears of parting are truth, goodness, beauty.
Tears of parting are Buddha, Moses, Jeanne d'Arc.

11 : *Blocked Path*

Your face isn't the moon
but it crosses the mountains and waters to shine on me.
Why is my reach so short
that I can't touch your breast in front of me?

If you would come to me, why don't you?
It's not that I can't go to you,
but there's no ladder by the cliff,
there's no boat in the water.

Who took the ladder and destroyed the boat?
I'll place a ladder of gems, make a boat of pearls.
I yearn for you who can't come to me
because the path is blocked.

12 : *Natural Virtue*

I don't wait for you because I want to
but because I find myself waiting for you.
That is: waiting for you is love, not chastity.

Some laugh and call me an old-fashioned woman
    guarding a petty virtue,
but it's not that I don't understand these times.
I don't aspire to make deep statements about life and virtue;
I don't rashly deny the sanctity of free love.
Once I tried to be natural and to live freely.

But in the end we say and do as we like.
As I wait for you I grow fat on anguish and tall on sadness.
My virtue is a "natural virtue."

13 : *Let Us Be One*

If you take my heart, take me too and make me one with you.
If not, give me your heart not just the heartache, and be one with me.
If not, send back my heart and give me unhappiness.
Then I'll have my heart and love the pain you give.

14 : *Ferryboat and Traveler*

I'm the ferryboat;
you're the traveler.

You walk on me with muddy feet;
I hold you and cross the water.
I bear you across the deep, the shallow, the rapid.

If you don't come, I endure wind, snow, rain,
and wait for you, from dusk to dawn.
Once you cross the water, you leave without looking back.
Sooner or later you'll come, I know.
I wait for you and grow old day by day.

I'm the ferryboat;
you're the traveler.

15 : *Rather*

Come to me. If you don't come, I'd rather you go.
This coming and going drains my life without giving me death.

If you reproach me, I'd rather you do it loudly.
Don't reproach me in silence—silent reproaches pierce me
　　like a needle of ice.

If you don't look at me, I'd rather you close your eyes.
Don't look askance at me—sidelong glances wrap a gift of thorns
　　in the cloth of love.

16   *My Song*

My song has no fixed rhythm,
so it has nothing in common with normal tunes.
This doesn't grieve me,
because my song should be different.

Melody smooths out the defect of songs.
Melody grinds up unnatural songs with human delusions.
To set genuine song to music dishonors its nature.
Music blemishes my song, just as making up your face disfigures it.

My song makes the god of love cry.
My song squeezes youth into rare, pure water.
My song enters your ear and becomes heaven's music;
It enters your dream and becomes tears.

I know you hear my song across the distant fields and mountains.
When its pitch stumbles and falls silent,
my song enters your sad, quiet thoughts and vanishes.
When I think of you listening to my song,
my heart pounds with exhilaration and draws out the notes of silence.

17 : *But for You*

But for you, why does this smooth, plump face fold into wrinkles?
But for missing you, I would be ageless until the end of time.
I would remain as we were in our first embrace.
Old age, sickness, death—because of you I don't hate them.
Give me life or death as you will.
I am but you.

18 : *Sleepless Dream*

One night I dreamt without sleeping:
"Where's my love? I'm going to see her.
Kŏm, take the path that leads to her and give it to me."
  "The path on which you go is the one on which she comes.
  If I take it and give it to you, she cannot come."
"As long as I go, it will not matter if she does not come."
  "If I give you her path, she'll come another way.
  You won't meet her on your course."
"Then take this path and give it to my love."
  "It makes no difference whom I give it to.
  Each person has his own path."
"Then how will I meet her?"
  "Give yourself to your path.
  Keep going without rest."
"There are too many peaks and rivers.
I cannot go."
  "Then I'll let you hold your love," Kŏm replied.
I held her with all my might.
My arms pressed my chest until it hurt,
but the emptiness they divided reunited in their wake.

19 : *Life*

Anchor and rudder lost, the small boat of life drifts on violent water.
A thread of hope from the dream of an undiscovered golden land
becomes a compass, a chart, a fair wind to sail the frightening sea
that beats against the sky on one end, against the earth on the other.

My love, hold tight this small life I give you.
Press it close, and in that sacred land the splinters of this sacrificed life
will become the rarest of jewels, which I'll fit together piece by piece
and hang upon you as an emblem of love.

My love, take my life, a small bird in an endless desert
without a single tree to perch upon, and hold it tight.
And then lift each crushed fragment of life to your lips.

The more joy and beauty there is, the better.
But, it seems, the less of your love there is, the better.
Your love exists between you and me.
To know the quantity of love,
we can only measure the distance between us.
If the distance is great, then the degree of love is great;
if the distance is small, the degree of love is small.
So small love makes me smile, great love makes me cry.

Who says when a person goes far away,
that love also goes far?
If your absence makes love distant,
what is this crying day after day if not love?

21 : *Pearl*

Once, I went to the seashore and gathered shells.
You gathered up my skirt, saying it would be muddied.
Returning home, you said I was like a child, playing with shells.
Then you went out and bought me a diamond, you did.

That day I plucked a pearl from an oyster
and put it in your pocket.
Where is that pearl?
Why do you let others see it?

22 : *Samadhi of Sorrow*

Death, clean as the blue light of heaven, cleanses all things.
Quiet night—the light of void—reigns over the earth.
By a faint candle, I lie so alone and resolute.
On a sea of tears I released a flower boat.
It carried my love and sunk without a sound.
Through the samadhi of sorrow, I attained "self void."

Drunk on flower mist, the beautiful girl
staggers along the vast plain of youth.
Regarding death lighter than a feather,
love's madman drinks the heart's fire like it's ice.

You loser in love, sick on love,
urging your love to kill itself—
hold me if you want satisfaction.
Don't you know that my arms embody that love?

23 : *Don't Doubt*

Don't doubt. Don't doubt even a little, though I'm far from you.
I don't mind if you do, but it only adds to your pain.

When I first held you, I shed my clothes of deceit
and presented myself naked as when I first entered the world.
Even now I offer myself as that first time.

If this seems unnatural, it is only because I want to
give you my guileless self forever.
If it's your will, I'll shed even the clothes of life.

If I have a fault, it's the "sorrow" of longing for you.
Because when you left, you pressed my lips over and over,
saying, "Don't be sad."

So forgive me this.
Sorrow for you is my very life.
If you don't forgive me, I'll take a shower of punishment
like falling petals in the spring morning rain.
I won't refuse the lash of your love.
I'll accept the bind of love's harsh law.

If you doubt me, then your error of doubt
and my fault of sorrow will cancel each other.
Don't doubt, though I'm far from you.
Don't add to your pain.

24 : *You*

Why smile when you look at me?
I want to see your frowning face.
I don't want to frown at you, though.
You wouldn't want to see it.
When the falling peach blossoms grazed your lips,
I cried, not knowing that my brow was creasing.
And so I hid my face with a gold-embroidered handkerchief.

25 : *Happiness*

I love you and I love your happiness.
I want everyone to love you and love your happiness.
And yet, I would hate the person who loves you too.
Hating that person is one part of my love for you.
And so, the pain of hating is my happiness.

If everyone in the world were to hate you,
I would hate them beyond measure.
If everyone in the world neither loved nor hated you,
that would be my unbearable pain.
If everyone in the world hated me because they loved you,
my happiness couldn't be greater.
The deeper their hate for me, the greater my love for you.

26 : *Misrecognition*

Come down, I'm terrified.
Why do you dance so high on that bough?
Hold tight to that limb and carefully, gently come down;
the leaves are going to brush your lotus-bud lips.

The half moon hung on the willow branches smiles faintly in reply:
"It's not that I don't want to come down, but, as you know,
I am *nim* to everyone. I don't want to refuse your fragrant call."

Without even a blade of grass, I clutched my naked shame,
stole quickly into bed and closed my eyes.
The half moon walked softly over,
hid outside my window, and looked into my eyes.
My shamed heart suddenly shuddered with fright.

27 : *Quiet Night*

The night is quiet and my room freshly washed.
Beside the folded quilt, I sit tending the fire.
I don't know the lateness of the night.
The flames have burned to cold ash,
but my loving heart hasn't cooled.
Before the cock crowed, we met and talked,
but dreams are vague.

28 : *Secrets*

Secrets? Secrets, you say. What kind of secrets would I have?
I tried to keep a secret from you, but it couldn't be guarded.

Through my tears my secret entered your eyes.
Through my breath my secret entered your ears.
Through my beating heart, my secret entered your touch.
Another secret became a splinter of red heart and entered your dream.

There is one last secret.
This secret is like a soundless echo and cannot be expressed.

29 : *Love's Existence*

Love, once called *love*, already isn't love.

Where is the word that can name it?

Can it be touched by rosy lips smiling faintly in anguish?

Can it be lighted by autumn eyes reflecting dark sorrow behind its tears?

Does it exist beyond shadowless clouds, echoless precipices,

    and the sea that the mind can't reach?

That land has no boundaries. A lifespan has no time.

The presence of love cannot be known through eyes or mind.

Love's secret is known only through your embroidery needle,

    your planted flowers, in your sleep, and in the poet's imagination.

30 : *Dreams and Cares*

Last night my cares lasted so long
I thought my dreams as long.
So I set off to see you
but awoke before reaching halfway.

At dawn my dreams were so short
I thought my cares as short.
But worry after worry—
I don't know when it will end.

My love, if you also
have dreams and cares,
I would rather that your cares
turn into dreams and dreams into cares.

31 : *Wine*

I made wine from fragrant grapes ripened by autumn breeze
  and morning sun.
The perfume of fermenting wine dyes the fall sky.
I fill a lotus leaf with this wine and offer it to you.
Take it from my shaking hands and wet your parched lips.

If kept overnight, this wine will turn to tears.
After one night more, my tears will turn to new wine.

32 : *Slander*

There's a lot of slander and envy in this world.
If there is any toward you, don't listen.
Those who pleasure in slander are glad that the sun has its spots.
They might slander you for having nothing to slander.

One can call a dozing lion a dead lamb,
but they can't call you coward for falling among thieves
   in the wilderness.
One can call lewd the goose sleeping with the seagull on the sand,
but they can't call you loose for being tricked into the brothel.
If there is slander and envy toward you, don't listen.

33 : "?"

Dim and drowsy, I heard your brisk steps,
Fighting heavy eyelids, I opened the window and looked:
wind-driven showers drive past the mountain ridge;
the sound of raindrops on the plantain leaves rises in waves.
At the moment emotion and reason collide,
the devil in humanity and the angel in beasts appear then vanish.
The young ape sleeps in the shaking clatter of your song.
It is awakened from its pitiful dream by the sound of falling flowers.
The jeweled flickers of the lonely lamp that guards the dead night
    quietly falls under its own weight.
Pitiable souls, burning in insane flames,
search out a new world in the hopeless freeze of despair.

It's the flower of the desert,
it's the full moon of the moonless night,
it's your face.
My jade-white lips can't touch yours, awash in a faint smile.
The window weighted by the moon's still light
    frames the bobbing shadow of a cat smoothing its coat.
Is it the Buddha or the devil? Is life but dust or a dream of gold?
Oh, little bird, sleeping on the frail branch that sways in the wind.

34 : *Your Touch*

Your love is hotter than flames that melt steel, but your touch
   is unbelievably cold.
I've known all kinds of coldness in this world, but nothing
   like your touch.
Your touch is colder than the fall wind scattering leaves
   on a frosty morning when chrysanthemums are in bloom.
Your touch is colder than the snow piled
   on ice on a keenly bright winter's night.
Your touch is colder than the monk's sermon, cool as sweet dew.

Without your touch, the flames that burn in me cannot end.
My heart is the only measure of the warmth of your touch.
Your love is hot enough to burn a mountain of cares
   and to dry up a sea of regrets,
but your touch is cold beyond measure.

35 : *Sweetbriers*

You said you would come before the sweetbriers' bloom.
It's already late spring.
Before spring arrived, I prayed it would come sooner;
but now that it's here, I'm afraid it has come too early.

The innocent children clamored to tell me
    the sweetbriers are blooming on the hill,
but I pretended not to hear.
The cruel spring wind blew the petals onto my dressing table.
Absently I touched a flower to my lips and asked,
"When did you bloom?"
It didn't reply—reflected through my tears, the flower became two,
    then three.

36 : *I Saw You*

You left and I can't forget.
The fault is mine, not yours.

Without any land to till, there's no harvest.
With nothing to eat I went to a neighboring house for potatoes and millet,
But its master said, *"Beggars have no humanity.*
Those without humanity have no life.
It would be a crime to help you."
As I was returning home, through my streaming tears, I saw you.

I have no home; I'm not counted on the census.
"The uncounted have no rights.
With no rights, what virtue can you have?"
asked the general who tried to violate me.
I resisted, and as my hatred turned to sorrow, I saw you.

Yes, I understand ethics, morality, law
   are nothing but the smoke worshipping the sword and gold.
Shall I accept eternal love?
Shall I blot out the first pages of human history?
Shall I take to drink?
As I wavered, I saw you.

37 : *Rain*

Rain has the greatest power and offers the best opportunities.
Rain blocks the sun, the sky, and others' prying eyes—
　　but not the lightning or rainbow.

I became a lightning bolt and rode the rainbow to you
　　for love's embrace.
If I quietly come on a rainy day and bring home your silence,
　　your lover will never know.
If you come on a rainy day, I'll send you a coat of lotus leaves.
If you come wearing the coat on a rainy day,
　　no one in the world will know.
If you quietly come on a rainy day and take away my tears,
　　it'll be an eternal secret.
Rain has the greatest power and offers the best opportunities.

38 : *Submission*

Others love their freedom, but I prefer submission.
It's not that I don't know freedom,
I just want to submit to you.
Willing submission is sweeter than exalted freedom.

If you tell me to submit to someone else,
that's the only thing to which I can't submit.
If I submit to someone else, I can't submit to you.

39 : *Bear with Me*

I have no choice but to leave; bear with this parting.
When you go over the ridge, don't look back.
My being is about to enter a grain of sand.

If you can't bear with this parting, bear with my death.
My lifeboat is sinking in a sea of shame.
Blow, make it drown quickly, and be glad for it.

If you can't bear my death, don't favor me with love.
Instead, make yourself unloveable.
I'll enter your heart and live in you.
Bear becoming one with me.
Love me not and I shall not love you.

Your signless love circles my youth like a faintly swaying gauze curtain
    that wraps itself around a young girl's dream.
Pulsating—young bloods dance to heaven's clear music.
Panting—little souls sleep in the shade of heaven's falling flowers.

Endless threads of attachment bind my sleep,
    as spring rain turns to blue haze amid the drooping willows.
A short dream struggles under the quilt, trying to follow the wind.
Desperate dream-cries stifle my throat, calling to people
    across the river.
Shattered moonbeams splinter dew-wet flowers like broken rice,
    and the bitterness of your parting turns into a sharp knife
    that cuts me to the bone.
The stream outside the gate doesn't need my tears
    to swell its flow.
The mad wind in the spring hills waits for my sighs
and gathers strength to shake the flowers.

41 : *Passion's Sky, Sorrow's Sea*

The autumn sky is high
but cannot rival passion's sky.
The spring sea is deep
but cannot sound sorrow's sea.

It's not that I dislike
the height of passion's sky;
but my reach is low
and I cannot climb.

I'm not ill at ease
with the depth of sorrow's sea,
but my legs are short
and I cannot cross.

If my reach increased and I could climb,
passion-sky's beauty would equal its height.
If my legs grew long and I could cross,
sorrow-sea's splendor would deepen its drop.

Were passion's sky to collapse
and sorrow's sea to dry,
I'd rather sink into that water
and fall into that sky.

I had thought passion's sky high,
but it's lower than your brow.
I had thought sorrow's sea deep,
but it drops below your knees.

My reach is low, my legs are short.
But to attain passion's sky and cross sorrow's sea
your arms are all I need.

Don't.

Don't look at me and pretend not to see.

Don't.

Don't seal your lips and speak with your eyes.

Don't.

Don't cry in cool embarrassment after smiling
    in the warmth of love.

Don't.

Don't tremble with excitement when picking the flowers of the world.

Don't.

A smile is dancing in the breast of my destiny.

Don't be timid all over again.

43 : *Master's Sermon*

I heard the Master's sermon:
"Don't be bound to the chains of love and suffer.
Cut the ties and your mind will find joy."

That Master is quite the fool.
To be bound with ties of love is painful, but to cut them
    is more painful than death.
In the tight bind of love's ties lies its unbinding.
Thus great liberation lies in bondage.
My love, I feared that the ties that bind me to you might be weak,
    so I've doubled the strands of my love.

44 : *Seeing Her Off*

She's leaving.
She doesn't want to go, and I don't want to send her away.
But she's leaving.
I had thought beautiful her red lips, white teeth, and fine brows,
but her departing cloud of hair, willowy waist, and pearl-smooth heels
    are more so.

Step by step she grows distant—now out of sight, now seen.
The further she gets, the closer our hearts;
The closer our hearts, the further is she.
I thought I saw her waving kerchief, but it was a slip of cloud
    smaller than a flying gull.

45 : *Diamond Mountains*

O, twelve thousand peaks—
Do you know where your love is and what he does?
Because of you, he's destroying religion, philosophy, reputation, wealth—
Everything, in the burning flames of his heart.

Are you the red of flowers?
The green in leaves?
Are you the drunkenness of tinted maples?
The awakening in white snow?

I know your silence well.
I know your calm, bemused smile
  suppressed amid the unending praise of eager children.

Heaven or hell—why can't you be just one?
Like dreamless sleep, be pure and simple.
I'm not a madman trying to pick flowers across the river with a short hook.
I too want peace and simplicity.
I kiss the slip of cloud borne by your breath.

O, twelve thousand peaks,
You don't know where your love is and what he does.

46 : *Your Face*

It's not quite right to call your face pretty.
Prettiness is a matter of human faces,
but your beauty exceeds humanity.

It's hard to fathom how nature gave such beauty to a person.
I know: it's because there's no match for you in nature.

What lotus flower can compare to your lips?
Where is the white jade that matches your complexion?
Have spring-lake ripples like your glances ever been seen?
Has morning light like the scent of your smile ever been heard?
Heaven's music is the echo of your song.
Exquisite stars are the forms of your eyes.

I am your shadow.
Only your shadow can match you.
It's not quite right to call your face pretty.

47 : *Planting a Willow*

I planted a willow tree in the garden
to bind my lover's horse.
But he snapped a branch and made a whip
to speed his horse away.

I would make a whip from every branch,
and urge my horse behind him.
But the countless limbs of the willow
tie down my bitterness.

48 : *Paradise in the Thornbush*

The spring air is beautiful.
It flows down from the plum branch I thought dead,
its beadlike buds nourished by the melting snow.
In another patch of sky, do you know an unknown fragrance
    flows from decaying snow bringing death to all flowers?
The clouds are thin; the stream is shallow; the autumn hills are empty.
But between gaunt rocks, the red maple flames in brilliance.
It too sings and cries.
Do you know such "life of nature" is given by the mature shade
    of summer
and disappears into memory in autumn's wind?

A blade of grass becomes the six-foot golden Buddha,
and the six-foot golden Buddha becomes a blade of grass.
The entire world is one nest, and all things a little bird.
I saw life reflected in the mirror of nature.
I was happy to leave you to tend the garden of joy
behind the thornbush of pain.

49 : *Is It True?*

Is it true? My love, don't deceive me.
Did the ones who took you from me say, "You have no lover"?
Do you cry in secret, but in front of them change your tears to smiles?
It's hard to endure tears, but to force them into smiles
   tastes more bitter than death.
Then I cannot help but defend myself.
I'll pluck all the blossoms of my life, make a garland for your neck
   and shout,
 "This is my lover's beloved!"

Is it true? My love, don't deceive me.
Did the ones who took you from me say, "We'll find you a lover"?
Did you then protest, "I'll remain alone"?
Then I cannot help but take revenge:
I'll mix my thin blood with my hot tears,
   water their bloodthirsty sword and shout,
 "This is my lover's beloved!"

I left my old home and met spring in another village.
Sometimes my dreams follow the spring breeze and reach a distant ruin.
My walking stick and my shadow chase each other,
    smeared with the green hue of grass.

On the path, I see flowers whose names I don't know—
I'll sit and perhaps forget my cares.
I thought the flower clusters were still wet with morning dew,
    but they knew first that my tears were falling.

51 : *Hymn of Praise*

You are gold tempered a hundred times over.
Bask in the love of heaven until the mulberry roots turn to coral.
Nim, my beloved, you are the first ray of morning light.

You know the weight of righteousness and the lightness of gold.
Sow the seeds of fortune in beggars' poor soil.
Nim, my beloved, you are the whisper of the old Paulownia.

You favor spring, light, and peace.
Become the bodhisattva that sprinkles tears on the heart of the weak.
Nim, my beloved, you are the spring wind upon a sea of ice.

Namgang River flows day and night but still remains.
In wind and rain Ch'oksŏk Pavilion stands vacant and flees
    with the arrow of time.
Non'gae, my love, you make me laugh and cry at once.
You are a fine flower that bloomed on the grave of Chosŏn;
your fragrance doesn't decay.
As a poet, I've become your lover.

Where are you? You're undying but can't be found in this world.
I think of your life, fragrant and sad like a flower cut by a golden knife.
Your gentle song, choking on the smell of wine,
wrung tears from the corrupt swords in prison.
A terrifying chill swirled your dancing sleeves;
it reached the flower beds in the land of the dead and froze
    the setting sun.
Your delicate heart was calm, but more chilling than had you trembled.
Your guileless eyes were smiling, but were sadder than had they cried.
Turning from red to blue then white,
were your lips the smile of the morning cloud?
The crying of evening rain?
The secret of the moon at dusk?
The sign of dew?

The flowers unplucked by your jewel hands reddened with shame.
The prints of your jade-white heels on the riverbank
   have been covered by the green of arrogant old moss.

Your house is an empty tomb, but I still call it your home.
Without a house even in name, I have no way of calling you.
I'm fond of flowers, but can't pick the ones blooming on your grave.
If I did, my insides would be plucked out first.
I'm fond of flowers, but can't plant them on your grave.
If I did, thorns would be planted in my heart first.

Forgive me, Non'gae. It is I, not you, who broke our pledge.
Forgive me, Non'gae. It is you, not I, who wept bitterly in your solitary bed.
Even if I wrote "love" in golden letters on my heart
   and raised it as a monument,
what comfort would it give you?
Even if I branded a melody of tears upon my song
   and rang it as a memorial bell,
what absolution would it give me?
One unforgettable pledge—no other woman will have my love.
Forgive me, Non'gae.
If you do, even the faults I have kept from the gods will vanish.

Non'gae, you live a thousand autumns.
Non'gae, you last not even a day.
So joyful am I to love you, and so sad.
My laughter brims over and becomes tears;
my tears overflow and become laughter.
Forgive me, my beloved Non'gae.

53 : *Remorse*

When I had you, I wasn't devoted.
My piety greater than my love,
my caution outran my joy.
Moreover, being cold in nature and hounded by poverty,
I didn't ease you in illness.
Now that you're gone,
tears of regret are greater than the distress of separation.

54 : *Love's Reasons*

It's not for nothing that I love you.
Others love my rosy complexion, but you love my gray hair.

It's not for nothing that I long for you.
Others love my smile, but you love my tears.

It's not for nothing that I wait for you.
Others love my vigor, but you love my death.

55 : *Your Letter*

Your letter has come, they said, so I left my hoe in the flowerbed
    and tore the letter open.
Though the hand was fine and the lines long, it said little.
Your letter would have said more with even fewer lines.

Your letter has come, they said, so I laid aside my needlework
    and tore the letter open.
Though it asked after me, it didn't say when you'd come.
Your letter would have told your arrival, even without pleasantries.

Your letter has come, they said, so I stopped infusing my herbs
    and tore the letter open.
That letter bore the address of a foreign warship.
Your letter would have stated your departure, even had you remained.

56 : *False Separation*

Do you remember when we parted?
We can comfort ourselves and say it's a false separation,
   but in fact our lips can't touch.
When will this false separation be over?
One, maybe two years, I can't say they don't matter.
How many times will the fading peach in my cheeks
   be touched by the heartless spring wind and turn to fallen flowers?
How much will the graying blue-black clouds behind my ears
   be bleached by the autumn sun and turn to white snow?
The hair whitens, but the heart reddens.
The blood cools, but the tears burn.
Love's hills are washed away, but in hope's sea the waves dance.

I only know one day this false separation will end.
That day will take our separation with one hand
   and bring death with the other.

57 : *If It's a Dream*

If love's bondage is a dream,
then so is liberation from the world.
If laughter and tears are dreams,
then so is the illumination of no-mind.
If the laws of all creation are a dream,
then I'll attain immortality in the dream of love.

58 : *Looking at the Moon*

The moon was bright and I yearned for you so.
Smoothing my bedclothes, I went in the garden and gazed awhile
   at the moon.

Slowly, it became your face;
I could clearly see your broad brow, round nose, and fine mustache.
A year ago, I thought your face was like the moon;
Tonight the moon has become your face.

Since your face is the moon, so is mine.
But do you know that my face has become the waning moon?
Since your face is the moon, so is mine.

59 : *Law of Causality*

You're breaking our promise and leaving.
How much truth did it have?
I can't accept this parting.
I know this parting will return to that promise.
This is the inviolate law of causality.
When you leave, I'll wait for your returning kiss to come
    before your parting kiss has dried.

I know there's no malice in your leaving
and your broken promise.
Even if you never quit this separation,
    my lips touched yours and will never know another.

60 : *Sleep Talk*

"What is love? For the sincere it requires no tears, no laughter.
Kick and crush love's gourd.
Bury tears and laughter in the dust.
Pound reason and sentiment into powder.
Ascend the height of emptiness and dance dizzily, sing madly.
Ply your lover and Satan alike with wine.
Become an idiot, a lunatic, a dead man living."

"You mean, love won't let go, even if it means your death?
Then, hitch a cart to its tail.
Ride it around as you like; rest if you want; sleep if you will;
    live or die as you please."

"It's ludicrous to stake yourself to love and then cry over it.
No one goes around with '*nim*' branded on their forehead.
Love is free, virtue is fluid, marriage is a thicket of rites."

All of this I cried loudly in my sleep.
My lover's smile is like starlight, unvanquished by the rays of blackness.
Before I knew it, the tears that racked my dreams had wet my pillow.
Forgive me, my love.
It's the fault of dreaming, but if you want to punish don't punish dreams.

61 : *To Kyewŏrhyang*

Kyewŏrhyang, you sleep in a bed of earth,
your beautiful and frightening smile still alive.
I mourn for your humanity and love your cruelty.

The fishermen of the Taedong River hear your song;
the revelers on Mount Moran see your face.
The children cry your living name;
the poets sing your bygone shadow.

We are fated to die, regretting what's undone.
What are your regrets?
You keep silent.

Your regret's redness turns into a brilliant sunset,
    blocking the sky and reversing the bleakness of falling day.
Your sorrow's blueness lengthens into willow threads,
    tethering the departing spring from its destined path.

I'll catch the morning sun on a golden tray,
fold the new spring into an apricot branch
    and lay them gently where you sleep.
They'll remain one night or last the winter,
    my beloved Kyewŏrhyang.

62 : *Satisfaction*

Is there satisfaction in the world?
Is there satisfaction in life?
If so, there must be some for me.

There may be satisfaction in the world, but it's one step ahead.
Its distance exceeds my reach, its speed matches my stride.
It can't be caught, it can't be thrown away.

Attaining satisfaction is dissatisfaction; it's always one step ahead.
Satisfaction is for the fool and the saint, or it's the expectation
   of the weak.
Satisfaction flows abreast with life.
I'd rather turn around and stamp out its traces.

I've attained satisfaction.
When shimmering dreams and goldspun illusions
   enveloped you in your flower garden,
I attained it.

63 : *Inverse Proportion*

Is your voice silence?
When you're not singing, I hear your song's melody clearly.
Your voice is silence.

Is your face darkness?
When I close my eyes, I see your face distinctly.
Your face is darkness.

Is your shadow light?
When the moon sets, your shadow shines on the dark window.
Your shadow is light.

64 : *Tears*

No one's crazy enough to think tears are pearls—
that's crazier than to mistake blood for rubies.
This is the rambling of the loser in love at a dark crossroad;
or the twisted words of a demented poet.
If tears are pearls, I'll bury all pearls in the dust,
except for the keepsake ring you gave me.

I've never seen jade ornamented with tears;
I've never seen tears drunk like wine at banquets of peace.
No one's foolish enough to think tears are pearls.
No—the tears you give me are tears of pearl.
I'll cry tears of pearl for you until my shadow leaves my body.
Every day, I hear the sighing jade flute in the immortal land of tears.
My tears form countless streams, and each tear is a creation.

Tear's jewels; sigh's spring wind; peerless treasures sanctifying
   love's ground!
When will love be perfected by tears that flood space and time?

65 : *Everywhere*

In the morning I put water in the basin to wash,
and you become the ripples caressing my reflection like a helpless child.
I wander the blooming hillside to forget my cares,
and you become the spring breeze lightly scenting my languid heart.
Unable to wait for you any longer, I lie in bed,
and you become a silent, dark light tenderly covering my shame.

You are everywhere I look,
so I closed my eyes and searched above the clouds and beneath the seas.
You become a smile hidden in my mind;
kissing my closed eyes, you tease, "Can you see me?"

66 : *His Parting Face*

Flowers are sweetest when they fall,
the sun most fine when it sets.
Melodies are best when choked,
his face most enticing when we part.

After parting, the face reflected in my fantasy is so bewitching
   I can't look at it without a cushion of tears.
I'll chisel that enticing face in my mind's eye:
a face too unfeeling to move me, it cannot stir my heart to love.
To lose sight of that charming face would pain me more than tears
   of sorrow.

67 : *First Love*

Who were the first lovers and when did they meet?
Who were the first lovers and when did they part?
Were the first to meet the first to part, or was it another pair?

I think the first lovers to meet were the first lovers to part.
Meeting without parting—that's not love, it is myself.
Parting without meeting again—that's not love, it is a passerby.
When we meet love, we worry about parting;
   and when we part, we pledge to meet again.
This is the legacy of the first lovers' parting.

Hence, not meeting is not love, and not parting is not love.
Meeting love gives me smiles, parting from love gives me tears.
Parting tears are better than meeting smiles;
   smiles upon meeting again are better than parting tears.
When will we share meeting-again smiles?

68 : *Cuckoo*

The cuckoo cries its heart out.
It cries and when it can cry no more,
it cries blood.

The bitterness of parting is not yours alone.
I cannot cry even though I want to.
I'm not a cuckoo, and that bitterness can't be helped either.

The heartless cuckoo:
I have nowhere to return, and yet it cries,
"Better turn back, better turn back."

69 : *My Dream*

When you stroll in the tree shade in the fresh of dawn,
my dream becomes a small star keeping watch above you.

When you nap on a summer's day flushed with heat,
my dream becomes a refreshing breeze swirling around you.

When you sit in solitude reading on a quiet autumn night,
my dream becomes a cricket chirping under your desk.

70 : *When Crying*

Flower-bloom mornings, moonlit evenings, rainy nights—
    these are the times you long for your lover, people say.
I too have cried much during such quiet times.

But then, I cry even more when people gather to talk and laugh.
Those with lovers try to comfort me with kind words,
    but such consolations sound like mockery.
At such times, I choke back the tears and make them flow down inside.

My friend, you make me weep like flowers blooming on the grave
    of a lost lover.
You gladden me like love met unexpectedly in desert darkness
    without a single bird.
You're the scent of blanched bones that break out of an ancient grave,
    floating skyward.
You're a song of hope within despair, sung while picking fallen flowers
    for a garland.

My friend, you weep over broken love.
Your tears can't bring back scattered flowers to the bough.
Sprinkle your tears beneath flowering trees, not on fallen flowers.

You say the scent of death is sweet, but you can't kiss the lips
    of dry bones.
Don't spread a web of golden song over that grave,
    but plant a bloodstained banner.
The spring breeze tells how the poet's song stirs the dead earth.

My friend, when I hear your song I'm unspeakably ashamed—
    because I hear it alone, far from my beloved.

I finished sewing all your clothes.
I sewed your scholar's coat, your suit, your pajamas—
   all but the embroidery on a small satchel.

That satchel is stained by my fingers—
   because I worked it, then worked it again.
Others suppose that I have little talent for needlework, but only I know
   this secret:
when my heart aches I embroider.
My heart follows the golden thread through the eye of the needle
   and from the embroidery comes a pure song that becomes my heart.
And still there are no valuables in the world worth carrying
   in this little satchel.

I haven't finished the satchel—
not because I can't, but because I like to embroider.

73 : *Love's Fire*

The fire that consumes all things was set by Suin.
The fire in me, dancing to youth's music, was set by my parting lover.

O water, that flows in the Namgang River,
your swirling blue breast lulled Non'gae's youth to sleep.
O Taedong River, circling Nŭngna Island,
you cursed the heartlessness of Kyewŏrhyang.
I call you both out of poetic habit,
but you have no power to douse the scorching flame.
If you can put out the fire inside me,
why is your throat too choked to sing a lover's song of yearning?
I see the flames blazing in your own heart that others don't see.

When my lover's tears join my cries,
I'll use the first drop to extinguish my heart
    and the second to sprinkle upon your breast.

74 : *I Love "Love"*

Your face is a quiet star in the spring sky.
But there are faces like the crescent moon
    that appear between the clouds.
If I love only charming faces,
why do I embroider a star instead of the moon on my pillow?

Your heart is flawless jade.
But there are hearts that are steady, brilliant, and hard like gems.
If I love only sublime hearts,
why do I set my ring with jade instead of jewels?

Your poem is a golden willow with new buds unfolding
    in the spring rain.
But there are poems like blooming lilies on an oily black sea.
If I love only fine letters,
why do I sing of willows instead of flowers?

When no one else loved me, you did.
I love not only you; I love your love.

75 : *If Not Forsaken*

When I lie in bed, sleeping then waking, waking then sleeping,
a lone lamp watches the night like a faithful guard.
If you don't forsake me,
I'll become life's lamp to keep watch over you a hundred years.

When I sit at my desk reading this and that,
the words obligingly yield good stories, pure songs, solemn lessons.
If you don't forsake me,
I'll become a reliable primer to suit your fancy.

When I see my lips in the mirror awaiting your kiss,
the faithful mirror smiles as I smile, frowns as I frown.
If you don't forsake me,
I'll become the heart's mirror and faithfully share your pain
    and pleasure.

When you left, I was sick in another village
   and there was no parting kiss.
It was the time of the first autumn wind,
   a leaf or two reddening on the maple branch.

I'm going to cut away your parting from eternal time.
Then time will be in two pieces.
You hold one end, I the other, and time will link
   when we join hands.

Then those poised to write the misfortunes of others
   won't be able to record your parting.
I'm going to cut away your parting from eternal time.

77 : *Magic*

You snatched away my joy like the autumn floods
   that sweep away the leaves piled in the small stream.
Now all I have is the pain.
But I can't bring myself to hate you
   because you eased me before you left.
If you robbed me of joy and pain at the same time,
I would have no heart at all.

I'm a star in the sky that hides its face in a veil of clouds.
I'm a pearl in the sea that becomes a button on your shoe.
If you take the star and pearl as your lovers, accept them with joy.
But if your heart is also troubled, let it be your pain.
But don't teach me the magic of snatching away hearts;
and then this separation won't be the end of love.

78 : *Your Heart*

I've seen the blackness of your brow and the shapeliness of your ears.
But I haven't seen your heart.
When you wrapped the large red apple you picked for me,
I saw your heart go in it.

I've seen your round belly and your slender waist.
But I haven't seen your heart.
When you saw my picture next to that of another woman,
I saw the greenness of your heart.

I've seen the whiteness of your nails and the curve of your heels.
But I haven't seen your heart.
When you put my jeweled ring in your pocket as you left,
I saw your heart hiding behind the ring, covering its face.

79 : *Summer Nights Are Long*

When you were here, winter nights were short;
now that you're gone, summer nights are long.
I thought my calendar was mistaken,
but the fireflies are streaming and the insects cry.
I know now whence the long nights come and where they go.
They come from the first wave of sorrow's sea, turn into sad music,
   a vast desert,
and finally disappear through despair's fortress into a demon's smile.

But if you come back, I'll take love's knife
   and cut the night into a thousand pieces.
When you were here, winter nights were short;
now that you're gone, summer nights are long.

80 : *Meditation*

The small boat of infinite meditation is cast adrift
　　on surging moonlit waves.
It crosses a distant land of stars until it reaches
　　a place of unknown name.
In this land, a child's smile, spring morning, and the sound of the sea
　　blend together to become a person.
In this land, people don't know the royal seal;
they trample thoughtlessly upon gold,
　　and don't know to love a beauty's youth.
The people of this land love laughter and the blue sky.

I moor the boat of meditation in this land.
The people clasp my hands and urge me to stay,
but I return to build a heavenly land in my lover's heart,
　　should he come back.
The moonlit waves with beaded crests sway in time
　　to the dancing grass.

81 : *Double Seventh*

"*Rather than living without you, I'll become somebody else,*
but not the Weaver Girl in the sky...,"
I once said coquettishly, searching your eyes.
In these words there is a sympathy:
How can the Weaver Girl bear to meet her Herdsman but once a year,
   on the seventh day of the seventh month?
In these words there is a conceit:
a vow to be preoccupied always by your kisses,
like a butterfly drunk on peonies.

The future is hard to know, vows difficult to keep.
The Double Seventh has passed ten times and more since you held me.
The Weaver Girl and Herdsman look at me with pity, but no gloating.

Night after night, they look across the Silver River and talk to each other.
On its banks, they splash water and relive regrets.
They recline with their feet in the water and sing songs,
pretending not to see each other.
They inscribe reed boats and blow them across to each other.
Reading them, they act like they don't understand.
When it's time to go, they say nothing and smile at each other.

It's now the evening of the Double Seventh.
They wear lotus robes pleated with orchid thread.
They sport laurel beads that shine with the seven colors.
Their cheeks flush in anticipation of drunken kisses,
overcome by the heat of their own happiness.
As they cross the Magpie Bridge, they pause to check
      their trailing robes.
They cross and in their embrace, tears and laughter know no order.
The future is hard to know, vows difficult to keep.

Their love is a display.
There is no way to show true love.
They cannot see my love.
The sacredness of love is not in display but in secrecy.
If they waved me to join them, I would not go.
It's now the evening of the Double Seventh.

The sound of an unconscious sigh turns into the spring wind;
dewy flowers bloom in the mirror that reflects my haggard face.
Around me, my only consolation is the breath of wind.
Unending tears turn into crystal that illumines the sanctuary
     of pure sorrow.
If not for these crystal tears, I'd have nothing to treasure in this world.

Breath of wind, crystal tears:
these are the harvest of my mourning.
Aching sorrow turns into strength and fire,
and like a young lamb, breathes into life.
The sighs and tears my lover gives me are the beautiful art of life.

83 : *Flower Fight*

Planting azaleas, you said, *"Let's have a flower-fight when they bloom."*
The flowers have bloomed and are fading.
Aren't you coming? Have you forgotten your words?

Red blossoms in one hand, white ones in the other, I start the battle.
You're the winner and I lose.
When we meet for the real contest,
I'll have the red blossoms and you the white—
then you'll lose to me each time.
Not because I like to win, but because you like to let me.
Each time I win I'll ask for the winner's prize,
then you'll smile at me and touch your lips to my cheek.

The flowers have bloomed and are fading.
Aren't you coming? Have you forgotten your words?

84 : *Playing the Kŏmun'go*

I play the *kŏmun'go* under the moon to forget my sadness,
but before the first tune fades, tears obscure my view.
The night becomes the sea; the harp strings a rainbow.
The sound of the *kŏmun'go* rises and falls,
and your swaying follows the pitch of the strings.
The last strains chase the night and fade into the dark of the elm tree;
you look at me listlessly and close your distant eyes.
You follow the fading tune of the harp and close your distant eyes.

85 : *Come*

Come, please come. It's time.
Do you know when you're supposed to come?
The time to come is when I'm waiting.

Come in to my garden, the flowers are blooming there.
Should anyone chase you, hide in the blossoms.
I'll turn into a butterfly and light upon the ones you hide among.
Then your pursuer won't find you.
Come, please come. It's time.

Come in to my arms, my breast is soft there.
Should anyone chase you, sink your head into my breast.
Though I'm soft as water, I'm a golden sword and iron shield
    to protect you.
Should my breast be like petals trampled by horses,
    your head still won't fall.
Then your pursuer won't touch you.
Come, please come. It's time.

Come in to my death, my death is always ready for you.
Should anyone chase you, stand behind my death.
In death, emptiness and omnipotence are one.
Love's death is at once infinite, everlasting.
In death, battleship and fortress become dust.
In death, the strong and the weak are companions.
Then your pursuer won't catch you.
Come, please come. It's time.

86 : *Pleasure*

My love, do you think I thrive, just as when you were here?
Then you can't say you know me.

Since you went so far away, I haven't had as much joy
   as the trace of a lone goose flying across the moonless sky.

When I look in the mirror, the smiles no longer come.
I no longer tend and water the flowering trees.
I hate even the sound of the quiet moon's shadow
   that crosses softly over to my thin window.
I find no sweetness in the fresh grove
   after a shower overruns the scorching summer sky.
I have no companions or playthings.

Since you left, I have one bittersweet pleasure in this world:
that's to cry my fill now and then.

87 : *Waiting*

You have me waiting day after day.
When the setting sun casts mountain shadows over the village,
I go beyond the grove to wait in desperate hope.
The children drive the oxen home, their reed flutes stifled with music.
The birds return to distant trees, swimming in the evening smoke.
The woods stand quietly, having sported with the wind.
This is a sign of its sympathy for me.
When the gravel path lies in darkness, following the stream
   I retrace my idle steps, leaving fading sighs in the quiet, distant sky.

You have me waiting day after day.
When darkness consumes the thin light of dusk,
I stand vacantly at the gate to wait.
The returning stars sparkle with a joyful look
   and nod their heads in greeting.
The insects in the grass make a peaceful night with their strange songs,
and lay to rest the battles of the day.
Mocked by the deceitful wind that rustles the lotus leaves in the pond,
my distant thoughts change into sharp resentment.

You have me waiting day after day.
When the relentless pace of time drives all hope away,
I lie in my desolate bed and wait.
The pressure point in my heart has caused storms in life's sea,
and the three thousand worlds have been washed away.
The pitiable butterfly, friendless and fading,
has suffocated in the forest of desire.
Noble philosophy has succumbed to the samadhi of tears.
My waiting has failed to find me, and in the end forgets itself.

Yes, I'm coming. I'm coming right now.
Oops! I was going to light a candle but I stuck the taper in upside down.
They'll make fun of me, now.
My love, I'm busy like that.
You scold me for being lazy.
Just look: *"Being busy is laziness,"* you say.
Why should I be bothered by your scolding?
I only worry that your *kŏmun'go* is out of tune.

My love, it's not the moon but the dawn that crosses the skyless sea
    to erase the shadow of the elm tree.
The cock in his roost is flapping his wings.
The horse in the stable is pawing the ground.
Yes, I'm coming. I'm coming now.

Postscript: To the Reader

Readers, I'm embarrassed to present myself as a poet to you.
As you read my poems, I know you'll be disappointed,
   with good reason.
I don't want your children to read them.
That would be like sitting in a flowering glade in late spring
   and rubbing a dry chrysanthemum to one's nose.

I don't know how late the night is.
The heavy shadows over Mount Sŏrak are thinning.
As I wait for the dawn bell, I lay down my brush.

—*8th Month, 29th Day, 1925*

Manhae and the Art of Poetry

I N THE OPENING DECADES of the twentieth century, the Korean Buddhist monk Han Yongun (1879–1944), known also as Manhae ("Ten Thousand Seas"), addressed his readers in the postscript of the present work, claiming "I'm embarrassed to present myself as a poet to you." Manhae did not think of himself as a poet, but like many Buddhist monks before him, he had a weakness for versifying. Consider the following poem, "Mountain Cottage Dawn":

> Arising, snow flies outside the window
> and blankets the mountain—dawn now.
> The cozy village homes are like a picture—
> A surge of poetic feeling, and even illness is forgotten.

This poem is a testimonial to the practice of the classic monk-poet, particularly within the Chan / Zen (Sŏn in Korean) tradition. Enveloped in nature's cradle, his moment-by-moment awakening to life is enacted through and captured in the words of poetry. Manhae's vivid mindfulness of the scene outside his window turns everyday perception into art—the village homes are "like a picture," and this awakening is embodied as poetic inspiration which overcomes the bodily afflictions that threaten to deaden his sensibilities.

Manhae composed poetry in both Chinese and Korean. There are 164 surviving Chinese poems, composed over a thirty-year period (1909–39), of which "Mountain Cottage Dawn" is one. Of his Korean poems, the majority are featured in the present work, *The Silence of Everything Yearned For*. Consisting of ninety poems, it was written during the summer of 1925 at the Paektam Buddhist temple in the Sŏrak Mountains, where Manhae was ordained as a monk in 1905. Manhae's current poetic fame in Korea is based upon this collection of poems.

Silence consists of love poetry. The first poem, "My Lover's Silence," narrates the lover's departure and establishes the enduring themes of the work: the happiness of meeting, the sadness of separation, the agony of longing and waiting, and most of all, the suffering of love perfected in the absence of the beloved.

Understandably, the identity of Manhae's lover, or in the Korean language *nim,* has been the subject of much speculation. In surprising contrast to the erotic language of *Silence,* Koreans have long favored the decidedly unromantic allegorical reading of *nim* as Manhae's native country, which at the time had been "lost" to Japanese colonial rule (1910–45). This highly abstracted political interpretation has been justified by persistent misreadings of Manhae's much noted preface to *Silence,* which appears to encourage allegorical interpretations of the poems:

> "*Nim*" is not only a human lover but everything yearned for.
> All beings are *nim* for the Buddha, and philosophy is the *nim* of Kant.
> The spring rain is *nim* for the rose, and Italy is the *nim* of Mazzini.
> *Nim* is what I love, but it also loves me.

Manhae's insistence on the semantic open-endedness of *nim* follows traditional Korean usage, in which *nim* can signify not only a "lover" in the romantic and erotic sense but also anyone or anything that is held in loving esteem—one's political sovereign, parent, teacher; one's country, humanity, God. Manhae's preface picks out religion, in addition to philosophy and politics. For this reason, the strongest argument against the political reading of *nim,* to date, has been the Buddhist one, which insists that the meaning of *nim* is actually the religious goal of enlightenment. Although the semantic reading of *nim* differs, the religious interpretation is quite similar to the political one in presuming that Manhae's "lover" is allegorical.

The propensity toward such abstract construals of *nim* diminishes one of the most notable aspects of *Silence*—its highly concrete and physical sensuality. Take, for example, poem 31, "Wine":

> I made wine from fragrant grapes ripened by autumn breeze and
>   morning sun.
> The perfume of fermenting wine dyes the fall sky.
> I fill a lotus leaf with this wine and offer it to you.
> Take it from my shaking hands and wet your parched lips.
>
> If kept overnight, this wine will turn to tears.
> After one night more, my tears will turn to new wine.

The scent of fermenting grapes that paints the autumnal sky leads to a tremulous offering that looks forward to an erotic fulfillment. The love of God (and perhaps of nation) has been conceived in such opulent terms in the literatures of the world, particularly in the traditions of religious poetry that use the human language of desire to express the insatiable longing for God. Buddhist enlightenment however, which lacks a personal God, is never envisioned in such terms in Asian poetry.

The presumption of this volume is that the point of poetry is to experience and appreciate the surface level of its words and images. The passion and agony that Manhae expresses for his beloved do not signify anything other than what his immediate words convey. The semantic openness of *nim* does not command one to take its overt language and replace it with something more distant, and Manhae's preface does not invite the reader to decide between more or less important manifestations of *nim*. Rather, Manhae states that all avenues of human activity, in their historical and passionate particularity, form the paths to human perfection and, paradoxically, to human transcendence. The preface reflects Manhae's own range of commitments, as reflected in his lifelong pursuits of Buddhist salvation, social reform, and political independence. These activities have been the focus of much scholarship, but very little attention has been given to Manhae's personal life, which included two marriages. The first marriage, in 1892, was by traditional arrangement, when Manhae was only thirteen years of age, and it was effectively abandoned when Manhae entered the Buddhist life at the age of eighteen. The second one occurred much later, in 1933, certainly as an active choice that put into practice his belief that clerical celibacy was a historical custom that no longer made sense. By this time, the clerical prohibition against marriage had already been abolished (in 1926), in concession to the growing practice.[1] Rumor also has it that during the time that *Silence* was composed, Manhae was quite enamored of an attractive nun of the

Sinhŭng Temple who made frequent visits to Paektam-sa for worship.[2] Given the absence of definitive documentation, however, the question of the subject of Manhae's *Silence* can be settled only by taking its words and feelings at face value.

Quite helpfully, Manhae elsewhere offers an explicit understanding of Sŏn Buddhism as it applies to life. In his own words, "Sŏn is not something limited to Buddhism, it is universal." Sŏn is not religious belief, doctrine, meditation, or the extinction of mind, he elaborates, but rather the very ordinary and necessary activities of life.[3] With such sentiment, Manhae faithfully reiterates the rhetoric of the original Chan masters of China, such as Linji Yixuan (d. 866, called Rinzai in Japanese), famous for their iconoclastic insistence that Buddhism is "nothing special."[4] What Manhae adds, however, is a particular emphasis on the body and sensory experience as the way to "see one's nature," or to become a Buddha.[5] Sŏn means the entire self, Manhae says, and when the self is experienced according to Sŏn, the self becomes the "highest of art."

Sensory experience arises from engagement with the world, and most acutely from the sensual realm of love. Sensual love inspires and reconstitutes itself as poetic art. When such art and experience entails the devotion of the entire being, such as Manhae's love in *Silence,* it is also religion because such love transcends mere gratification and personal history. As we will see, Manhae speaks of this process, which begins with particular and concrete personal experience but becomes much more. It will be useful to see how this principle—this form of art making—worked in his well-documented public life. We will approach the matter by first considering Manhae's political persona—the one that gives rise to the persistent readings of *Silence* as a lament for the lost sovereignty of Korea.

The Politics of Poetry

Manhae's political life might well be understood through the inherently political nature of literature itself, not only in the early twentieth century, but throughout the history of East Asia. To begin, the sole fact that Manhae composed *Silence* in Korean rather than literary Chinese, and in free verse rather than in traditional regulated form, makes a political statement. Manhae embraced the campaign to adopt the Korean script *(han'gŭl)* as a substitute for Chinese, which had been the lingua franca of the elite since the sixth century. This campaign was a main staging ground for Korean nationalist sentiment at the turn of the century. The poetry of *Silence,* moreover, is colloquial and exhibits the natural rhythms of the Korean language, as well as the peculiarities of Manhae's regional dialect. In these respects, Manhae's modernist political consciousness is quite evident.

Literary practice often forms the culture-specific moments of social and political change. In this particular era, Korean history paralleled the contemporaneous New Culture Movement in China, which displaced literary Chinese with the more accessible *baihua*, or spoken Chinese, as the written medium. The *han'gŭl* movement in Korea similarly unified the written with the spoken language of the nation. Although the *han'gŭl* script was invented in the fifteenth century at the command of King Sejong (r. 1418–50), the scholar class suppressed it. In 1896 a group of political progressives founded *Tongnip sinmun* *("The Independent"),* a newspaper that published entirely in *han'gŭl*, in a colloquial prose style. Hence, language reform signaled a new and modern national consciousness, along with the formation of a new brand of intellectual. In the past, the politics of poetry was an erudite affair confined to the record keeping and letter writing of scholar-officials in the king's court. The modernism of Manhae's era lies in the conversion of literature and letters into a mass medium, and into a way of addressing a national, reform-minded audience. The mass politicization of literature was not limited to poetry but also embraced the new fiction, which was published in serial form in proliferating newspapers and magazines.[6]

Another factor in the nationalistic reading of *nim* is the prominence of Manhae's political profile as a result of his central participation in the March First Independence Movement (Samil Undong) of 1919. Like China's May Fourth Movement of the same year, the event was directly connected to international developments in the wake of the First World War. Woodrow Wilson's principle of national self-determination during the postwar peace settlement was ultimately applied only to Eastern Europe, but it could not help but raise the hopes of those in East Asia. In January 1919 Korean expatriates in Shanghai sent a representative to the peace conference in Paris to make an international appeal for Korean independence. The mission was a failure, but the momentum for independence led to an official Korean Declaration of Independence, drafted by the poet Ch'oe Namsŏn and completed by Manhae, who also took the lead in enlisting thirty-two religious leaders to sign it. Its public declaration in Seoul on March First triggered demonstrations throughout the country, involving some two million students, farmers, laborers, and shopkeepers.

For his part in the March First Movement, Manhae was imprisoned from 1919 until 1922. During his confinement, he penned a corpus of essays dealing with the question of Korean independence, largely in response to the interrogations of the Japanese prosecutor. The essays were smuggled out of Korea, where they reached expatriate Korean communities in Manchuria, Siberia, and China. "The objective of human life," he wrote, "is genuine freedom, and without it, there is no pleasure or happiness. In the effort to obtain independence, there is no matter to be regretted and one would gladly give up his own life…. To deprive the freedom of even one person injures the harmony of heaven and earth—what then can be said about the obliteration of the freedom of twenty million?"[7] This declaration is representative of Manhae's political liberalism, much of which was absorbed during his studies of Western thought while he was abroad in Tokyo in 1908. Moving from principle to concrete political considerations, Manhae presciently observes that without securing the independence of Korea, the peace of Asia and even the world is at stake. Japan's annexation of Korea is only a first step, he notes; next Japan will covet Manchuria and Mongolia, and it will dream of conquering the Chinese mainland.

By all accounts, Manhae was an uncompromising political figure, unrelenting in the face of Japanese pressure and unforgiving toward fellow patriots who eventually acquiesced to colonial rule—including Ch'oe Namsŏn, who ultimately did not sign his own Declaration of Independence. In this context, it is easy to see why Koreans have read *Silence* as Manhae's palpable lament over his lost country. This interpretation also reaches back to the premodern practice of allegorical writing in Chinese and Korean literature. Specifically, literature was used to describe familial and personal situations, but the underlying intention was to comment on matters of state. One common example is the trope of the virtuous wife who is wrongly maligned and cast out by her husband. Court officials often used this trope to assert their moral impeccability in the face of political disfavor.[8] Quite different from modern socially conscious literature, such allegory veiled personal grievances about specific events. Allegorical writing allowed the author to vent his resentments but to remain safe from censorship or political reprisal.

Popular lore has it that the Japanese colonial government suppressed *Silence* soon after its publication in 1926. Evidence for this is scanty, however, and it seems rather unlikely, given that *Silence* garnered little public attention during Manhae's life. The allegorical intention, in any case, seems out of keeping with the modern elements of *Silence*. To be sure, Manhae's political consciousness surfaces now and then, the most succinct example being his choice to date the completion of *Silence* to the fifteenth anniversary of the Japanese annexation of Korea (see his postscript, the poem "To the Reader").[9] The dating naturally reinforces the nationalistic perspective. The following interpretation of the lead poem, "My Lover's Silence," is an example of how poetry can be read as political comment. The original lines read:

> My love is gone.
> Ah, the one I love is gone.
> Crossing the narrow path to the maple grove that shatters
>   the mountain green,
> she tore away from me.
> Promises, like bright gold blossoms,
> turned into ash scattered by gentle wind.

The first line tells of the lover's departure, imaged as a sudden and abrupt breach in the midst of a vivid landscape. In one interpreter's reading, the lyrical evocation of scenic colors—the red of a maple grove that invades the greenery of mountainsides—is an allegorical occasion: The "mountain green" that is shattered by the "maple grove" is Korea. The maple grove itself, of course, is Japan. The fourth line continues this theme of figurative meaning: the "promises," or lovers' vows that shrivel to ash from the ardor of their original intentions and expectations are the vows of March First Independence Movement, which at the time of writing had come to naught.[10]

Silence was composed a short three years after Manhae's release from prison, when his political activism was at a peak.[11] Adding to this environment was the example of other poets, contemporaries of Manhae, who addressed Korea as *nim* in their compositions.[12] But not everyone has been persuaded by the political reading of *Silence*. Some have insisted on the abstract totality of *nim*, which can never be fully manifest and which endlessly transforms through the encounters of actual and historical experience.[13] Such a reading is rooted in Buddhist metaphysics, which embraces the opposites of form and formlessness and allows for the greatest possibility of referents. In line with this reading, *nim* is not a single referent but rather a mystical totality. In yet another Buddhist reading, *Silence* is an allegorical discourse on Buddhist enlightenment.[14]

In following Manhae's own Buddhist thought, however, the equality of all things means that the surface reality of words should not be supplanted by some hidden yet higher level of truth. On the other hand, the freedom proffered by the Sŏn principle of emptiness encourages one to use words in creative tension and self-contradictory ways. In Chan/Sŏn/Zen Buddhism, words are considered useful, even enlightening, when used playfully, but deadening when used pedantically. A chief feature of this playfulness is the use of paradox, in which words are used contradictorily as a way of saying something useful, as in poem 20, "Measure of Love":

> The more joy and beauty there is, the better.
> But it seems the less of your love there is, the better.
> Your love exists between you and me.
> To know the quantity of love, we can only measure the distance
>   between us.
> If the distance is great, then the degree of love is great;
> If the distance is small, the degree of love is small.
> So small love makes me smile, great love makes me cry.
>
> Who says that when a person goes far away,
> love also goes far away?
> If your absence makes love distant,
> what is this crying day after day if not love?

Manhae's vision of love is expressed through a paradoxical logic about the corresponding measures of distance and love. In all human affairs, our tendency is to focus on the peak moments of fulfillment, in contrast to the in-between spots—the valleys and flat spaces that make the heights possible. The happiness of love is normally associated with the moments of connection and consummation, obscuring the fact that such moments are relative to and hence dependent upon their opposites—separation and longing. The human reflex to cling to gratification and to avoid deprivation is futile because the two are interdependent. In the realm of human relationships, the inevitability of separation, both physical and emotional, is perhaps an inherently poetic theme.

Manhae's language plays upon the dynamics of interdependency, but what the words convey quite directly and simply is the longing of romantic love. This is true of the vast majority of the poems in *Silence*. A few selections, such as the homages to Non'gae and Kyewŏrhyang (poems 52 and 61, respectively), focus on political contexts, and these poems can also be read at face value. The lead poem, "My Lover's Silence," however, marks a moment of profound personal loss, "My love is gone. / Ah, the one I love is gone," and *Silence* thrashes between the poles of contemplative acceptance and tempestuous struggle with the pain that ensues. Some interpreters have discerned a narrative evolution that begins with the sorrow of separation and evolves through movements of acceptance, renewed hope, and finally reunion.[15] The first and last poems, "My Lover's Silence" and "The End of Love," do certainly mark narrative moments of separation and reunion that provide a frame. All of the poetry in between exhibits the diversity and richness of Manhae's historical moment, however, encouraging the reader to run with Manhae's multiplicity rather than to be weighed down by any master schema. A more useful approach is to deepen our view of Manhae's historical moment by considering the traditional relationship between Buddhism and poetry, which provides the context for Manhae's particular practices.

Buddhism and Poetry

In the history of East Asian Buddhism, the link between enlightenment and art has been consistently expressed through the transmutation of Buddhist practice into poetry. Beginning with the *gatha*, the four-line verse indigenous to Indian

Buddhist literature, the tradition of versifying Buddhist teachings expanded into East Asia. There, poetry was used by Buddhists to express the values and virtues of religious life, particularly the life of mountaintop seclusion. In addition, poetry was seen as a contemplative, spiritual practice in itself.

The best of Buddhist poetry in East Asia has flowed in tandem with a tradition of nature poetry characterized by persistent themes, most particularly the joys of the simple life in retirement from the world and the beauty of remote mountain vistas that symbolize spiritual endeavor and fulfillment. These themes originate in China, with Daoist-inspired distinctions between the rustic, natural realm of fishermen and humble craftsmen, who follow the true "way," and the cultural realm of emperors and ministers who dissipate their minds and their very lives in pursuit of political reputation. During the prolonged period of disorder between the fall of China's Han dynasty in 220 C.E. and the establishment of the Sui in 581, the marriage of neo-Daoism with Buddhist "emptiness" philosophy forged an indelible association between spiritual wisdom and the contemplation of nature, particularly through poetry. Daoism taught a way that nourished the self by aligning it with the greater movements of the natural world. Buddhist emptiness philosophy insisted that the ultimate insubstantiality of the phenomenal world was best understood through immersion in that world. For the men of letters who reeled from the breakdown of Confucian political society in this era, these religious lessons were best practiced within the idealized realm of nature, as a specific antidote to the chaotic "world of dust."

The themes that invoke these classic Buddho-Daoist values—the vicissitudes of the life of government service, the vanity of human endeavors, the joys of the simple pastoral life, are signified by a ready supply of imagery that served as raw materials for fresh poetic endeavors through the centuries. Thatched huts and brushwood gates, mountains and springs, white clouds, sedge capes and bamboo hats, poetry and wine—such objects are the inventory of this landscape:

> The birds and their chatter overwhelm me with feeling:
> At times like this I lie down in my straw hut.
> Cherries shine with crimson fire;
> Willows trail slender boughs.
> The morning sun pops from the jaws of blue peaks;
> Who ever thought I would leave the dusty world
> And come bounding up the southern slope of Cold Mountain?[16]

Han Shan (mid-seventh century) of China's Tang dynasty most famously ties Buddhist consciousness with landscape poetry. Immortalized in paintings as the quintessential Chan free spirit, Han Shan is the half-mad rustic sage who makes art of his life through his nonconformity and poetry. In addition to the traditional theme of retirement, this poem exemplifies the incomparable nature poetry for which East Asian poets are famed.

The links between nature, withdrawal from the world, and spiritual self-cultivation dominate the verses of Korean monk-poets as well. More significantly, the ideal of retirement is not a monopoly of the clerics but a poetic conceit shared by the literati who made up the ranks of government officials. The theme of withdrawal permeates the widespread vernacular song poems of Korea known as *sijo,* as well as the poetry composed in Chinese.[17]

Take, for example, the following verse by the famed minister and poet Chŏng Ch'ŏl (1537–94), in the court of King Sŏnjo (r. 1567–1608):

> Milky rain on the green hills,
> can you deceive me?
> A sedge cape and horsehair hat,
> can you deceive me?
> Yesterday I flung off my silk robe—
> I have nothing that will stain me.[18] (CA 99)

Or the following from the chief state counselor and established neo-Confucian scholar Sin Hŭm (1566–1628):

> Don't laugh if my roof beams
> are long or short, the pillars
> tilted or crooked, or my grass hut small.
> Moonlight that pours on the vines,
> the encircling hills,
> are mine—and mine alone. (CA 111)

For the high-ranking men of state, some of whom ultimately joined the community of Buddhist clerics, the turn to nature is an act of refuge from the fickle course of human affairs. Thus the moon is constant, as are the bamboo and pine in much poetic observation, and the person who enjoys "ownership" of what is free to all is the one who has realized the higher value of the natural world in conjunction with the natural self.

The flight of literati ministers such as Chŏng Ch'ŏl into political exile was a rather common fate in the faction-driven life of the Korean court. It was rarely permanent, however. Aside from the Buddhist clerics, for whom world renunciation was meant to be lifelong, the vast majority of the literati lived also within a Confucian world that emphasized the perfection of the individual through social and political order. In this world, the Buddho-Daoist ethos of world renunciation easily elided into the Confucian self-imagining of the "hidden sage" who retreated from court to await a better time to serve. Such retreats were hence temporary respites during the most vexatious periods of one's political career.

Even more commonly, however, the poetry of world renunciation functioned as a *mental* respite that combined the therapy of political protest with the cultured pursuit of aesthetic expression—a pursuit that was a requirement of political advancement. The literary output of such scholar-officials was a primary element of a contrapuntal harmony that embraced Buddhist transcendence, on the one hand, and Confucian self-establishment, on the other. In this manner, nature poetry signified the life and practice of actual monks throughout East Asian Buddhist history, but it also fed the self-imaginings of men who were quite entangled in the world and its affairs.

Manhae's Socially Engaged Buddhism

Manhae was a citizen of the modern world committed to social progress and human betterment. The literati of premodern China and Korea subsisted for centuries within a political and social order that prevailed even while the fortunes of individuals and dynasties vanished with the wind. Manhae, on the other hand, lived during the advent of a new world, in which a social Darwinian ethos mandated either adaptation or extinction. More specifically, Manhae was a denizen of a country abruptly torn from its past and reduced to a pawn of imperialism, which also brought with it the irreversible compass of internationalization.

As a Buddhist monk deeply engaged in his world, Manhae advocated the "demolition" of the past and amply utilized the language of Western political liberalism, including hints of socialism. More importantly, however, the foundation of his social engagement reached back to the "mind-only" philosophy of Yogācāra Buddhism, as well as to Sŏn Buddhist thought. This is not to suggest, however, that Manhae surpassed the traditional tension between Buddhist transcendence and Confucian social commitment by substituting a new alliance between Buddhism and political modernism. Rather, Manhae recaptured traditional Buddhist thought in order to respond to his unprecedented historical circumstances, in action as well as in words. In this, what Manhae articulated was quite traditional—the Indian Mahāyāna text, the Vimalakīrti Sutra, for example, had long articulated the ideal of the Buddha who acts in the world. Manhae's esteem for this iconic scripture of East Asian Buddhism is conveyed by his Korean translation, which he started in 1933. What is notable about Manhae's life is the degree to which he realized this Buddhist call to action in the world beyond a mere rhetorical affirmation. For this reason, he can be called one of the first "engaged Buddhists" of the twentieth century.[19]

Manhae understands the essential point of Buddhism to be the teaching that all is mind: All phenomenal experiences are created by mental factors that have been conditioned by personal history. The deluded person mistakes the resulting experiences for "reality" itself, when in truth they are emanations of mind.

As such, phenomenal reality is multivalent in its appearance but unified in its empty or non-ultimate character. This "one in all and all in one" philosophy entails that no mind-manifested category, including that of "Buddha" or "enlightenment," stands outside of the essential unity and ultimate equality of all things. As Manhae states, "The hallmark of Buddhism is equality. According to Buddha, every being and thing is possessed of Buddha nature, and this is equality."[20] Buddha nature is another way of speaking of the emptiness of all things. This emptiness is not a negation—a philosophical nihilism that denies existence or value. Rather, it is a philosophy of freedom based on the observation that "reality," as a mind manifestation, is really no different from the liberation of nirvana. Manhae elaborates: "Superficially, Buddhism advocates spiritualism, but the real view of Buddhism is that mind and matter cannot be independent of each other. Mind is itself matter (emptiness is form), matter is itself mind (form is emptiness)."[21] Manhae here uses the famous formula from the *Heart Sutra* that "form is emptiness and emptiness is form." Form means the worldly affairs that create the possibility of human attachment and delusion, but whose inherent emptiness can only be known *through* form rather than outside of it.

How did Manhae put his Buddhist thought into practice? In addition to his political activities, which have already been examined, we can also look at Manhae's attempts to reform Korean Buddhism itself. In his day, Manhae's voice was one of many calling for the revitalization of Buddhism and Buddhist institutions, which had suffered grievously under the formal oppressions of the Chosŏn dynasty (1392–1910). Korean Buddhists faced the twentieth century already weakened by centuries of persistent economic deprivation and persecution by a hostile neo-Confucian regime that stripped monasteries of their landholdings, decimated their rank and file, and reduced clerics to social pariahs by forbidding them to enter the capitol. Since the late nineteenth century, Korean Buddhism was further challenged by the growing presence of Japanese Buddhist sects and Christian missions. The educational and social outreach activities of the Christian churches, in particular, were phenomenally successful in winning Korean converts. By 1927, Japanese colonial census reports indicate that Korean Christians (Catholics and Protestants combined) had reached 265,000 in number, outnumbering the 189,800 Korean Buddhists.[22] This gap continued to grow throughout the colonial period. By the same year, Japanese Buddhism had established eighty-eight monasteries on Korean soil, representing nine different sects. Although these temples ministered primarily to Japanese laity who lived in Korea, they were organized like modern Christian churches and were active missionizing forces. In light of these foreign religious presences, the vitality and even survival of Korean Buddhism was a pressing concern of the Buddhist sangha.

Manhae's manifesto for reform is detailed in his *Reformation of Korean Buddhism, (Chosŏn Pulgyo yusillon)* completed in 1910 and published in 1913. Here Manhae's systematic arguments and positions stand in contrast to those of his compatriots. Most Buddhist reformers of this time embraced "cultural nationalism," which dealt with the colonial situation by seeking gradual evolution toward modernization and national self-sufficiency. This orientation ironically sanctioned a cooperative attitude toward the Japanese, who were also the source of Western liberal learning on which cultural nationalism was based. Manhae's *Restoration of Korean Buddhism,* on the other hand, is notable for its radical orientation, seen in its rhetoric of cultural demolition and its desire for immediate structural revolutions.

In later writings, particularly in the magazine *Pulgyo* (Buddhism), which he edited during the 1930s, Manhae explicitly condemned the Japanese regime's control of Korean temples, which reduced them into bureaucratic units of the colonial administration. Instead, Manhae championed *minjung* Buddhism, or Buddhism for the masses, utilizing a term that took on explicit socialist connotations in the 1920s. Manhae advocated a revolution in Buddhist organization and consciousness in order to liberate all beings, socially and economically as well as spiritually. Throughout his Buddhist life, Manhae labored to maintain the autonomy of Korean Buddhism from Japanese control, and to revive Buddhism as a moral and spiritual foundation for modern Korean life.

The reformist ferment of Manhae's Buddhist career was a direct response to his social and political location. Manhae's efforts, however, like those of his fellow reformers, ultimately yielded little fruit. The Buddhist reform movement was hopelessly divided against itself, strapped by a lack of financial resources and mocked by modern secularists within and outside its ranks. Colonial repression severely limited the practical efficacy of these reformers, and in the wake of the highly militarized rule of the 1930s, even the most ardent and youthful Buddhists leaders acquiesced to the political status quo. Manhae's own *minjung* Buddhism was never fully developed as an ideology, and Manhae never moved beyond intellectual effort to the level of grass-roots organization.

The failure of Manhae's activism in Buddhist institutional reform does not diminish the significance of his action in the world. For ultimately, Manhae's objective was not to promote organized Korean Buddhism as such, nor to champion the inherent good of particular social revolutions. For Manhae, the particularities of history are ultimately inseparable from the transcendence of religion. "Buddhist belief is belief in the self," Manhae otherwise states, and this self is something that is not separate from the rest of the world. "It is a self that penetrates others' selves and things. In other words, every person has the ability to individualize the universe and at the same time to universalize the individual."[23] The self arises with the rest of the world, and through individual activity, each person participates in the creation of the world. This creative activity is significant in the moral sense of the individual's responsibility for the world he or she engenders. On the other hand, religious enlightenment is predicated on individual actions that rise above limited personal and even historical interests, and for this reason the ultimate success or failure of action as defined by those limited contexts is of no consequence. Individualizing the universe means embracing what is at hand and responding to the particularities of the moment. Universalizing the individual, on the other hand, means rising above the illusion of the absolute necessity of one's historical imperatives. The trope of silence in Manhae's poetry suggests that the perfection of action is embodied in the silence of one's *nim*, which, in fact, is the failure to attain what one desires. Absence thus underscores the import of action, regardless of its historical outcome.

In a 1931 magazine interview, Manhae approaches this idea in response to the interviewer's questions about the political consciousness of Shakyamuni, the historical Buddha. The interviewer points out that even the Enlightened One could not transcend his race and culture—he wore Indian clothes, spoke an Indian tongue, and had Indian coloring. If the Buddha were a Korean alive today, the interviewer queries, could he sit idly by in the face of the current clash between China and Japan in Manchuria, the formation of the League of Nations, and current international economic affairs? The force of the interviewer's questions is to insist that if religion is to go beyond platitudes such as "love thy neighbor," then one must act within history, which entails prejudiced commitments rather than moral generalizations. Manhae responds, however, by insisting that political movements and revolutionary actions are not the equal of religion. "The truth of Buddhism lies in the well-being of all people," Manhae states; "the Buddha would not be concerned with saving only Koreans, he would not draw a distinction between national boundaries or blood."[24] If the Buddha helped Indians, it was because India provided his immediate environment—an expedient context for the truth that all beings are equal. The point of historical action, in Manhae's view, is that it provides the concrete setting for transcending the particular.

A turning point in Manhae's religious understanding and practice came while he was traveling abroad in Manchuria in 1911, shortly after the Japanese annexation. In an unfortunate but transforming incident, Manhae was mistaken by fellow Koreans for a Japanese spy and shot. As he lay bleeding to death, Manhae had a vision of the Bodhisattva Kwanŭm (Sanskrit: Avalokiteśvara; Chinese: Guanyin; Japanese: Kannon), the bodhisattva of compassion, who appeared to him as a beautiful young woman. Flinging her flower at him, she cried, "Your life exists in the twinkling of an eye! Why do you lay there so still?" Manhae credits this vision for bringing him back to life.[25] This story also offers the charter for Manhae's socially engaged Buddhism, which adheres to the command of Kwanŭm that is so tellingly narrated: As the excruciating pain of the gunshot wounds gives way to the pleasant numbness of a death swoon, Kwanŭm appears as a blissful and serene vision of calm. But rather than gracing his departure from the world, the bodhisattva jolts Manhae back to life with the command to take action in the world.

Manhae was a Buddhist activist for his entire life, lecturing, publishing, and making Buddhism accessible to ordinary people. His extensive *Buddhist Digest* (*Pulgyo taejŏn*), for example, is a thematically ordered abridgment of over fifteen hundred Buddhist texts, put into the Korean vernacular in order to convey the essential character of Buddhist teachings to a large audience. Manhae's greatest literary legacy, however, is his poetic practice, which reached its flowering with *The Silence of Everything Yearned For.* This legacy is far richer and more complex than the mere popularization of Buddhism through poetry. In poetry, Manhae found a medium that transcends the discourses of both doctrine and history. To wit, Manhae uses the language of art to move toward the spiritual goal of "universalizing the particular," and by doing so he transcends the particularities of his own social and intellectual location.

From History to Poetry

When *Silence* was first published in 1926, it attracted relatively little attention. Modern Korean poetry is commonly dated to the first decade of the twentieth century, when Ch'oe Namsŏn, the aforementioned author of the 1919 Declaration of Independence and the so-called "founder" of modern poetry, began to compose outside of conventional rhythmic forms. Korean literati followed Japan's and China's example of literary experimentation and modernization. This included the popularization of literature through the founding of literary magazines and monographs, thereby making literature accessible to a broad reading public. The publication in the 1920s of some seventeen collections by individual poets testifies to a flowering of the new poetry movement. Since the 1960s, Manhae's initial obscurity as a poet has been overcome by the enormous critical and popular success of *Silence*. Currently Manhae's *Silence* outshines its rival publications. Only Kim Sowŏl's collection of 127 poems, *Chindallae-kkot* (Azaleas), published in 1925, equals it in current esteem.

The delay in Manhae's literary fame stems in large part from his ambiguous relation to literary modernism. Because Manhae was not a self-styled poet, he felt less compulsion to jump aboard the bandwagon that sought to revolutionize poetry. More than half of his collected poems follow the traditional custom of composition in Chinese, and his Korean poems outside of *Silence* favor the well-established *sijo* format.[26] Although much is made of Manhae's modernism, such as his use of free verse in *Silence*, it is the accretion of the old and the new that creates Manhae's organic voice. His ability to keep the past alive was not a matter of principle but a natural function of his own identity betwixt and between two epochs. In one critic's appreciation, "it was precisely because of that close alliance with the past, that irrevocable linking of himself to the tradition and then working his changes, that Han Yong-un [Manhae] managed to create a poetry that was neither imitative nor derivative."[27]

The presence of the past in *Silence* can be glimpsed, indeed, through the persistence of nature imagery. The pastoral props of Paulownia and lotus leaves, flowers, apricot and willow branches, mountains, rivers, moon, stars, rain, and spring breezes lend a definite idyllic quality to Manhae's poetic landscape:

I left my old home and met spring in another village.
Sometimes my dreams follow the spring breeze and reach a distant ruin.
My walking stick and my shadow chase each other,
smeared with the green hue of grass.

On the path, I see flowers whose name I don't know—
I'll sit and perhaps forget my cares.
I thought the flower clusters were still wet with morning dew,
but they knew first that my tears were falling.

In poem 50, "The Flowers Knew First," the first stanza is reminiscent of traditional poetry in its natural descriptions and imagery. The second stanza injects overt human sentiment—falling tears—as nature poetry is wont to do, and yet the sentiment is delivered in a way that decenters the feeling subject: It is the flowers who call attention to the tears. Compare this poem with the following from Manhae's *sijo* collection:

An idle person in a mountain hut,
moved by pity for the autumn flowers,
cut down the fence
to let in the sun,
but the west wind blew in
and snapped off the blossoms.[28]

Both poems move to juxtapose nature with human sentiment. In this poem, the poet's pity for autumn flowers proves to be an irrelevant affair in the context of nature's inherent designs—the flowers are doomed with or without the poet's intervention. In this manner, the poem echoes the traditional theme of nature's inexorability and artlessness. In "The Flowers Knew First," Manhae dallies with the pathetic fallacy that the flowers know his sadness, but he overturns that expectation by revealing that the flowers merely provide a canvas for his own tears. Like much of the poetry of *Silence*, the poem reworks familiar poetic elements to fresh effect.

The past is also present in *Silence* through the echoes of past Korean poets—particularly courtesans. These voices are threaded through the more erotic moments of *Silence*, which vividly recount the experiences of separation, sorrow, yearning, and regret. "Pearl" and "Planting a Willow" (poems 21 and 47), with their respective emblems of devotion and abandonment, trace specific lineages to Hŏ Nansŏrhŏn (1563–89), a celebrated female poet of Chosŏn Korea. "When You Left" and "Summer Nights Are Long" (76 and 79) both borrow the poetic conceit of spacializing time from a singularly famous *sijo* poem by Hwang Chini (1506–44), a renowned courtesan. In addition to borrowing directly from famous female poets, Manhae frequently engages the traditional East Asian literary practice of speaking in the female voice. In some poems, this is made clear by explicit references to female objects and activities, such as "skirt" and "needlework." In other poems, female tone, language, and attitude are conveyed, although this is less obvious in translation.[29]

To turn to the modern side of *Silence*, the most significant influence on Manhae was not the Korean poets of his day but rather the Indian poet Rabindranath Tagore (1861–1941), who claimed the 1913 Nobel Prize for literature based on his poetic anthologies *The Gardener* and *Gitanjali* (Song Offerings). These anthologies were translated into Korean in the 1920s to much acclaim, and the poetry of *Silence* can be read in large part as a dialogue with Tagore. The Indian poet is one of three historical people directly addressed in *Silence* (the other two being the courtesans Non'gae and Kyewŏhyang). Poem 71, "Reading Tagore's Poem 'Gardenisto.'" offers explicit homage to Manhae's Indian muse, but Tagore's presence in the volume goes much deeper, permeating *Silence's* foundational structure and language. Manhae embraces Tagore's poetic language, most especially the vocabulary of "song" and "silence," which threads itself throughout *Gitanjali*. The length and thematic unity of *The Gardener,* which consists of eighty-five love poems, also serve as a model, as well as its idiosyncratic move of addressing its readers in the final poem. Additionally, Manhae derives his long prose style from Tagore, which no other Korean poet of the time duplicates.

Manhae's indebtedness to Tagore has proven a tricky path to negotiate in Korean critical scholarship, which invariably culminates in claims of Manhae's ultimate individuality and even superiority to his Indian muse. This jingoistic posture is blind to the poetic bounty created by Tagore's far-reaching presence in *Silence*. Interpreters tend to reduce Manhae's interest in Tagore to a focus on politics, and as a result they confine the connection between these two men to their shared status as citizens of Asian countries under colonial rule. This move is made primarily through a political interpretation of "Reading Tagore's Poem 'Gardenisto,'" which reads in part:

> You say the scent of death is sweet, but you can't kiss the lips of
>   dry bones.
> Don't spread a web of golden song over that grave; but plant a
>   bloodstained banner.

Here Manhae supposedly scolds Tagore for his indifference to politics, for his immersion in poetry at the cost of commitment to revolution.[30] The esteem Tagore enjoys in Korea as a Nobel Prize winner, bespeaks the vicarious satisfaction many Koreans felt in the West's admiration of an Asian. This satisfaction survives to the present day—the Tagore Society of Korea was founded as recently as 1981. Tagore's supposed political apathy, however, is easily parlayed into an unflattering contrast with Manhae. But it is difficult to attribute such a belief and intent to Manhae himself, based on the words of this poem alone. It is crucial to note that in this poem Manhae is responding to *The Gardener*, an anthology of love poems that seeks ultimate fulfillment in religious transcendence, which is attained in death. Tagore characteristically states:

> Love, my heart longs day and night for the meeting with you—
>> for the meeting that is like all-devouring death.
> Sweep me away like a storm; take everything I have; break open my
>> sleep and plunder my dreams. Rob me of my world.
> In that devastation, in the utter nakedness of spirit, let us become one
>> in beauty.
> Alas for my vain desire! Where is this hope for union except in thee,
>> my God?
>
> *(The Gardener 50)*

This death ultimately necessitates the silencing of song and poetry, expressed quite explicitly in *Gitanjali* 103: "Let all my songs gather together their diverse strains into a single current and flow to a sea of silence in one salutation to thee." This movement toward finality and silence is the pointed bone of contention in

Manhae's tribute. It is also the subtext of *Silence's* lead poem, "My Lover's Silence," in which Manhae declares that his own songs of love will wrap themselves around his *nim's* absence. Love is not fulfilled in death, Manhae proclaims, but rather in separation, which occasions life and art. Manhae's "bloodstained banner" is not the flag of political revolution but rather the emblem of all action. As so much of *Silence* conveys, death is not the final step or the ultimate fulfillment of love. Instead, real love and transcendence are attained through the endurance of absence that is fulfilled in art. Manhae's vital dialogue with Tagore at key points in *Silence*—the lead poem, the tribute in poem 71, and the postscript poem—evolves as a negotiation over the function and nature of such art, and of poetry itself.

If Manhae uses poetry to transcend politics, the elements of poetry are nevertheless also historical products. And yet, a key element of what Manhae maintains from the past is a literary practice that is indelibly marked as a spiritual exercise. Rather than taking refuge in traditional (or new) images and rhythms for their own sake, Manhae infuses his poetry with the vital signs of his own experience, and thus paradoxically rescues such personal poetry from the captivity of a single epoch. Manhae's spiritual exercise is realized as a fresh practice, one that resists reduction into one particular idiom—honoring the Sŏn ideal of "live words" whose meanings are endowed by history—but is never bound by it.

Silence seeks the transhistorical domain of art that speaks to all those who yearn. Manhae used all the literary forms close at hand, including political essays and serialized fiction. It is the poetry of *Silence,* however, that arises from the philosophical foundations of Buddhism to engage his particular historical commitments, and in turn to elevate them into a meditation on the universal dynamic of longing. *Silence* works through personal history to get beyond it to religious and aesthetic perception.

Manhae in Translation

Selections from Manhae's *Nim ŭi ch'immuk* are included quite regularly in anthologies of Korean poetry, but to date only three complete English translations have appeared. The earliest is offered by Younghill Kang and Francis Keely under the title *Meditations of the Lover*. This translation, aside from being unavailable, leaves much to be desired. It imposes an artificial poetic structure, deforming Manhae's natural prose into stanzas of highly staccato, elliptical verses. The rendering not only misrepresents and masks Manhae's prosodic style, which is one of the most notable aspects of *Silence,* but also leaves the meaning nearly indecipherable. Furthermore, the translation is quite liberal, frequently interposing lines and senses that are absent in the original.

The second translation is rendered by Sammy Edward Solberg in his doctoral dissertation, "The Nim ŭi Ch'immuk (Your Silence) of Han Yong-un, A Korean Poet." Twenty poems from Solberg's translation appear in *The Columbia Anthology of Modern Korean Poetry,* edited by David R. McCann. Solberg is quite faithful in maintaining the literal content of Manhae's poems, and his translation is accompanied by an excellent critical discussion. One can quibble, however, with a particular aspect of the translation, stemming from the academic nature of Solberg's work. The poetry of *Silence* is typically characterized by long, nonmetrical sentences that are notable for their free-flowing cadences in the original Korean. Solberg tends to be quite literal in his translations, which results in an English prose that is often overburdened. Nevertheless, I have consulted Solberg to great benefit in my work, and hence I recognize my indebtedness to him.

The third and most recent translation is yet another team effort, this time by Jaihiun Kim and Ronald B. Hatch. Presented under the title *Love's Silence*, this volume is the most aesthetically successful of the three, yielding many lovely and skillful translations from Korean into English. The volume takes a primarily literary approach, intending the poetry to stand on its own. Its renderings can sometimes be obscure, however. It also tends to abbreviate Manhae's original, often to good effect, but sometimes to the point of significantly altering the work. Alterations range from omitting lines to actually changing the meaning of a poem, perhaps inadvertently, perhaps intentionally. Kim and Hatch offer a two-page discussion of Manhae's life and a biographical chronology. A few poems carry footnotes about historical sites or figures. Sometimes they offer interpretive comments, mostly consisting of undocumented and unexplained symbolic readings of particular words. The sketchiness of background discussion and annotation does not help to illuminate the sense or context of the poems.

Here I have aimed for a translation that is faithful both in content and style. I am aware that translations are creations in their own right, and my hope is to extend Manhae's poetic legacy through the contemporary English language.

Nim ŭi ch'immuk was originally published by Hoedong Sŏgwan in May 1926. This first edition became extremely scarce and was reprinted in 1934. Since this original publication, Korean orthography has been standardized and hence modern editions offer a corrected version of Manhae's original spellings. The editions that I have consulted are from volume 1 of *Han Yongun chŏnjip* [Complete works of Han Yongun] and Han Kyejŏn's modern and original editions offered in his *Han Yongun ŭi nim ŭi ch'immuk*.

Notes on the Poems

Abbreviations:

CA   *Columbia Anthology of Traditional Korean Poetry*
HYC   *Han Yongun Chŏnjip*
RT   *The English Writings of Rabindranath Tagore*

"Preface: Idle Words"

Manhae's political consciousness is evident in his reference to Giuseppe Mazzini (1805–72), an internationally renowned Italian patriot whose career was devoted to the cause of Italian national unity and independence from Austrian and papal domination. His espousal of modern liberal principles such as republicanism, democracy, and the liberation of the masses exemplify the political ideals Manhae embraced when studying Western learning.

The statement that *nim* "also loves me," at the end of the first stanza, engages the Buddhist idea of dependent origination, or the belief that all things arise in relation to one another. This is particularly true of the subject-object relationship: the knowing subject gives rise to the known object, and the object also creates the knowing subject. The Buddha, for example, exists by virtue of all the sentient beings that he saves. Hence the one who loves and creates a *nim* is in turn created and loved by *nim*. The point is reiterated at the end of the second stanza: *nim* is one's shadow in the sense that it is created by the loving subject.

1. "My Lover's Silence"

This poem is the title piece for the entire collection in Korean. Here, however, I translate the title as "My Lover's Silence" instead of "The Silence of Everything Yearned For" in deference to the distinctness of this lead poem, whose *nim* is imaged as a human lover. A distinct shift occurs between the first two stanzas, in grammatical tense, as well as in sentiment. The first stanza dwells upon the parting of the lover, which is already past; the second uses the present tense to assert that separation from *nim* is not an end but rather a beginning. In this manner, the poem offers a rationale for the poetic art to follow.

The final line, "My common song of love wraps itself around my lover's silence," is quite certainly a response to the final poem of *Gitanjali* (Song offering) by Rabindranath Tagore (1861–1941), which states in part, "Let all my songs gather together their diverse strains into a single current and flow to a sea of silence in one salutation to thee" (RT 78). As Tagore prepares to "die into the deathless" union with God, his song offerings also merge into a final silence. In contrast, Manhae suggests that from the void of silence arises the phenomena of life and art. The "common song of love" in the last line is a translation of the literal and vague phrase "song of love that does not surpass melody (*kokcho*)." In poem 16, "My Song," Manhae uses *kokcho* again to refer to the standard tunes that fixed the meter for traditional *sijo* poetry. In that poem, Manhae differentiates his poetry, which does not follow the standard meter, from that of *sijo*. In this line, however, he seems to suggest that ultimately his poetry does not surpass the traditional song form. The void of silence, or emptiness, is the singular font of all art, which is what animates everything that is yearned for. The poetic connection between Manhae and the Indian poet Tagore is discussed in the historical essay at the end of this volume.

Finally, Manhae's use of the word "kiss" in the first stanza is worth noting. This English loan word was uncommon in the 1920s, and its foreignness is accentuated by the fact that the English sounds are spelled out phonetically (*k'i-sŭ*) in Korean. Its inclusion here, as well as in a number of other poems, lends Manhae a distinctively modern flavor. He might very well have been influenced by Korean translations of Tagore, whose references to kisses were phonetically rendered.

3. "I Don't Know"

The human and natural worlds are frequently juxtaposed in traditional East Asian poetry, creating a set of fixed associations and moods. Seasonal images— willow threads, red maple, bright moon, flying geese, the call of cuckoos—are painted in order to convey the poet's state of mind. In contrast to juxtapositions, however, Manhae tends to prefer equivalences. In this poem, all six lines pose copula metaphors in which a human feature is amalgamated with a natural entity: footfall = Paulownia leaf; face = blue sky; breath = fragrance; song = stream; poetry = setting sun; heart = lamp. The metaphors suggest metaphysical mysteries rather than simple comparisons, an idea that the title "I Don't

Know" reinforces. Human and natural phenomena are both linguistic creations that emerge from the single source of mind. The queries "Whose footfall?" "Whose face?" "Whose song?" suggest an ultimate inability to name this source that is the generator of all life.

The paradoxical assertion of the penultimate sentence, "After burning, embers become fuel again," parallels the logic of the *Heart Sutra*, in which form, or passion (which is commonly represented as fire), is emptiness; and emptiness, in turn, is reconstituted as form. The unnameable emptiness is the source of all life and of all names.

4. "I WANT TO FORGET"

The contradiction entailed in the attempt to forget is emphasized by the Korean word *saenggak*, which means both "to think" and "to remember." To think about forgetting, then, already enacts the moment of remembering. "I Want to Forget" is suggestive of the poem "Unforgettable" by Kim Sowŏl (1902–34), and it is the only poem in *Silence* that clearly exhibits the influence of a contemporary Korean poet. Although the theme of remembering and forgetting is an explicit connective thread between the two poems, the overall similarity is limited to the themes of love and separation. Sowŏl's "Unforgettable" is as follows (my translation):

> Unable to forget, you'll remember me.
> So the world goes; let it be
> And some day you'll forget.

Unable to forget, you'll remember me.
This is how time passes,
And more or less you'll forget.

Still you might protest:
"How can I not remember
The yearning that I cannot forget?"

5. "Don't Go"

This is the first poem in this collection with an overt political sense. The language of the poem suggests a woman addressing her husband or lover, pleading with him not to become enamored of the Japanese masters, with their false promises of modernization and prosperity. The Rose of Sharon mentioned in the first line of the second stanza is the national flower of Korea.

6. "Lonely Night"

The imagery of the third stanza—"illusion's queen," "golden sword," "celestial flowers"—is quite opaque. One can be guided in the reading of this poem by the reference to "empty mind" (*mushim*) at the beginning of the poem, which invokes the Buddhist belief that the world is a creation of mind. The universe/death and life/sleep juxtapositions in the second stanza suggest variations on the "being/nonbeing" polarity, which is basically a function of mind. The mind thinks the universe; without mind, there is no existence at all. The third stanza continues this theme: *kŭmsil*, or "golden thread," is homophonous with the word for conjugal harmony, suggesting that love's bliss disappears into the fold of "no mind." "Illusion's queen," which also vanishes, may very well be the self, which is illusory in Buddhism. The verb *chŏngsa,* translated as "to die for each other" in the last line of the stanza, actually means a lover's suicide. The topic, then, appears to be the mutual annihilation of self and love, accompanied by the religious realization that love and attachment are functions of mind that vanish with consciousness.

8. "Waking from a dream"

Meeting one's lover in a dream is a common trope of traditional Korean poetry, and subject to endless imaginative turns. The underlying idea is that in the absence of one's love, dream assignations—though ultimately unsatisfying—are perpetuated by the force of desire, as seen in the following verse by Pak Hyogwan (1850–80):

> She came to my dream,
> but was gone when I woke.
> Where has she gone leaving me,
> The one I long for?
> Dreams may be empty,
> but visit me as often as you can. (CA 142)

In the last two lines of the present poem, Manhae invokes the specter of lovers whose dream meeting is foiled because both are out in search of each other: "If your footsteps hadn't awakened me / I would be riding a cloud in search of you." This theme is realized by the poet and courtesan Hwang Chini (1506–44) in the following poem (my translation):

> With no path but the path of dreams,
> I go in search of my lover, he goes in search of me.
> Every night we pass each other in dreams—
> Could we but start together and meet along the way.

12. "Natural Virtue"

"Virtue" is a translation of *chŏngjo,* which customarily refers to female chastity. The restrictive norms of Confucian propriety forbade the remarriage of widows, including virgins whose betrothed died before marriage and consummation ever took place. The highly regulated and compulsory nature of traditional female virtue forms the contrast for the "natural" virtue spoken of here. The references to "free love" and "living naturally" are quite modern, and Manhae's support of the women's movement is exhibited in his essay "Women's Awareness" (HYC 1:284).

14. "Ferryboat and Traveler"

The image of the ferryboat is particularly evocative of the Buddhist analogy of the raft. The Buddha's teachings ferry beings from the shore of suffering to the shore of liberation. This poem fulfills Manhae's statement that all beings are the *nim* of Buddha. The poem speaks in the voice of a Buddha or Bodhisattva who dedicates him- or herself to the salvation of all beings. Orthodoxy states that both the Buddha and his teachings should be abandoned, however, upon reaching the far shore of liberation.

16. "My Song"

In the first line, Manhae declares that his poetry is not regulated in the traditional *sijo* meter. *Sijo* poetry was originally song lyric set to standard tunes. These tunes were typically broken into 4-4 or 3-4 syllable groupings, although variations are frequent. Hence all the references to "melody" or "music" (*kokcho*) in this poem refer to these tunes that determined the meter of *sijo* poetry. Free verse releases the poet from these forced rhythms. As a result, Manhae claims, the natural rhythm of his songs emerge, in contrast to inferior songs that take cover in standard tunes.

Compare the last line of the second stanza to Tagore's *Gitanjali* 7:

My song has put off her adornments. She has no pride of dress and decoration. Ornaments would mar our union; they would come between thee and me; their jingling would drown thy whispers.

My poet's vanity dies in shame before thy sight. O master poet, I have sat down at thy feet. Only let me make my life simple and straight, like a flute of reed for thee to fill with music.

(RT 44–45)

The similarity of metaphorical language contrasts with the difference in poetic object. *Gitanjali* is addressed to an absolute God whose voice would be obscured by human ornamentation. Manhae's unadorned songs, on the other hand, reveal the natural rhythm of language rather than the transcendent voice of God.

18. "Sleepless Dream"

Kŏm is a Korean folk god, apparently native to Manhae's Ch'ungch'ŏng Province.

The embrace of emptiness in the final line is clearly inspired by *The Gardener* 51:

> Then finish the last song and let us leave.
>   Forget this night when the night is no more.
> Whom do I try to clasp in my arms? Dreams can never be
>   made captive.
> My eager hands press emptiness to my heart and it bruises
>   my breast.
>
> (RT 107)

According to one interpreter, "Tagore suggests loss, negation. [Manhae] suggests fulfillment, affirmation—the void is his beloved" (Solberg 211).

22. "Samadhi of Sorrow"

"Samadhi" is the Buddhist Sanskrit term for meditative concentration. It signifies the meditative discipline that leads to the calming and emptying of mind. This emptying entails direct confrontation with and penetration of mental phenomena, and the process can be narrated as a dark and turbulent mental journey, as Manhae does here.

23. "Don't Doubt"

The metaphor of nakedness dominates this poem. In the last stanza of *The Gardener 56*, Tagore honors the nakedness exacted by love because one cannot find shelter from it:

> I hoped my love would be saved from the shivering shame of the shelterless, but you turn your face away. Yes, your path lies open before you, but you have cut off my return, and left me stripped naked before the world with its lidless eyes staring night and day.

(RT 110)

25. "Happiness"

The title of this poem appears to belie its content, which dwells primarily upon the emotion of hatred. The contradiction allows for an exploration of the dual nature of attachment, and the fact that love and hatred are positive and negative manifestations, respectively, of the single phenomenon of desire. Manhae makes this observation in the most carnal form, through the voice of a jealous lover: "I would hate the person who loves you too." Love is a form of discrimination that is defined in contrast to the hatred that is felt for the rival. But the phenomenon is far more complicated: "If everyone in the world neither loved nor hated you, / That would be my unbearable pain." One's attachment to the beloved demands the same of others; the most unbearable condition is the indifference of others towards one's love object. This mix of emotions—jealousy toward the rival and the demand that others share one's own attachment—reveals the fact that love and hatred are not opposites but rather the warp and woof of attachment.

To be sure, attachment is the nemesis of Buddhist enlightenment, and it is spelled out specifically as greed and hatred, which along with ignorance form the three roots of suffering in Buddhist doctrine. But as with so many of the poems in this collection, Manhae articulates love of *nim* as the forge that begets transcendence. In this poem, his self-awareness of the mutual dependency of love and hatred—"Hating that person is one part of my love for you. / And so, the pain of hating is my happiness"—suggests a power of direct observation that is the basis of enlightenment.

26. "MISRECOGNITION"

In this poem, the speaker mistakes the moon for his lover. In traditional nature poetry, the moon is sometimes referred to as one's companion. Sin Hŭm's poem is a classic delivery of the theme:

> Don't laugh if my roof beams
> are long or short, the pillars
> tilted or crooked, or my grass hut small.
> Moonlight that pours on the vines,
> the encircling hills,
> are mine—and mine alone.
>   (CA 111)

Sŏng Hon (1535–98) reverses the sentiment, recognizing that nature is partial to no one:

> The mountain is silent,
> the water without form.
> A clear breeze has no price,
> the bright moon no lover.
> Here, after their fashion,
> I will grow old in peace.
>   (CA 94)

Manhae's realization of the theme suggests that *nim*, like the moon itself, is not something to be possessed. The mood suggests an anxious and ominous dream, far from the serene, contemplative posture of the original poetic theme.

33. "?"

The question mark within quotation marks is Manhae's original title. The effect is a self-conscious ambiguity that echoes the title of poem 3, "I Don't Know." In that poem, the metaphysical mystery of the source of life is a key theme. The present poem suggests a dream experience, which is a frequent premise as well as topic of Manhae's poems. In East Asian Buddhist literature, the distinction between life and dream, in their putative separation as "reality" and "illusion," respectively, is constantly questioned. The penultimate line of this poem, "Is it the Buddha or the devil? Is life but dust, or a dream of gold?"

engages this dominant literary/religious theme. In tandem with the question mark title, the line ponders the presumed difference between conceptual oppositions—Buddha/devil, dust/gold, reality/illusion—as mental phenomena that are ultimately insubstantial. Poem 40, "Which is Real?," offers another title that underscores the theme of metaphysical ambiguity, and another poem that is comprised as a dream.

36. "I Saw You"

The *nim* of this poem is Korea, Manhae's native land lost to Japanese annexation. In the present land, natives are violated and rendered homeless by the occupiers. The final line proposes various paths of action, all exercised by Manhae during his lifetime. Acceptance of eternal love is entrusting oneself to Buddha; blotting the pages of human history is taking to revolution; taking to drink is embrace of modernism.

41. "Passion's Sky, Sorrow's Sea"

The "passion" of "passion's sea" evokes the classic Buddhist equation of passion with samsara, or suffering. The "sorrow" of "sorrow's sea" is a translation of *han,* which is predominantly associated with the political suffering of the Korean people. In Manhae's context, Japanese colonial occupation was the primary source of *han*, but it also alludes to the oppressions visited upon the people by Korea's own ruling elites. In the postcolonial era, *han* is associated with the political division of Korea into two ideologically and militarily opposed nations, as well as the succession of military regimes in the Republic of Korea from the 1960s through the 1980s.

43. "Master's Sermon"

The Master preaches a sermon of Buddhist world renunciation. Manhae's response represents a later Mahāyāna Buddhist attitude which recognizes that salvation is within the world. This poem displays the inversionary logic common to Sŏn/Zen, with its claim that freedom lies in the bondage to desire, or the very obstacle that poses the largest barrier to liberation in early Buddhist doctrine.

45. "Diamond Mountains"

The Diamond Mountains form the northern peaks (currently in North Korea) of the mountain range that runs down the center of the Korean peninsula. It is famed for its beauty and rugged scenery, and it is the subject of countless poetic tributes. Although mountains are traditionally associated with Buddhist hermitages and withdrawal from political life, here the lover or *nim* of the Diamond Mountains can also be interpreted as those devoted to the lost land of Korea—to wit, those like Manhae who are engaged in independence movements and revolutionary action. The polyvalency of the Diamond Mountains as a sign—as well as the polyvalency of Korea itself—is explicitly invoked by Manhae's yearning for the simplicity of meaning, a simplicity that is denied by the silence of the mountains.

46. "Your Face"

The word "forms" at the end of the third stanza ("Exquisite stars are the forms of your eyes") is a translation of the compound *hwahyŏn*, formed by two Chinese characters meaning "transformation" and "manifestation." This is not a common Korean word, being instead Mahāyāna Buddhist terminology that refers to the ability of Buddhas and bodhisattvas to assume any form in order to save sentient beings. The concept of phenomenal manifestation is fundamental to Mahāyāna Buddhism, signifying not only the compassion of Buddhas and the ideal of universal salvation, but also the metaphysical view that all phenomena are illusory and artistic manifestations.

Manhae's use of this technical term at the end of this stanza, which is formed by a progression of metaphors, is extremely suggestive. The first line considers, then rejects, the comparison of the lover's face to lotus flowers and jade, which are common signifiers of feminine beauty. The second line produces a more complex comparison between "lake ripples" and the lover's "glances," and then offers a pair of synesthetic metaphors about "hearing" the "morning light" that is like the "scent" of the lover's "smile." Even these comparisons are rejected, however, for the equation of "heaven's music" with the lover's "song," and "stars" with the lover's "eyes." The progression from mere simile to identity, and from hackneyed to complex, opaque imagery, yields a literary and philosophical statement. The result is a poem that is concerned with more than the peerless beauty of a human face. The real subject, as Manhae himself states, is a beauty that exceeds humanity, but which can be expressed only through bold and fresh literary art.

47. "Planting a Willow"

In traditional poetry, the threadlike branches of the willow tree furnish an image of the binding ties between lovers. Manhae utilized this image in the first line of the second stanza of poem 40, "Which is Real?": "Endless threads of attachment bind my sleep, / as spring rain turns to blue haze amid the drooping willows." Another variation on the theme is provided in "Heartless Willow," which Manhae assuredly knew. It was written by the courtesan Kyewŏrhyang, whom Manhae eulogizes in poem 61, "To Kyewŏrhyang." Her original poem is as follows (my translation):

> Departure in the darkening day by the Taedong River.
> The countless threads dangle gently from the willow tree
> And simply droop without binding my departing lover.

The association between willow threads and the bonds of love seems to be favored by women. In any case, Manhae uses the female voice in this poem. The double, four-line verse form that Manhae employs also suggests traditional Chinese-style poetry, matching a traditional theme to a traditional form.

49. "Is It True?"

The double signification of *nim* as both a lover and the people of Korea is suggested here. The overt language articulates the complaints of a woman addressing her lover, but the situation described resembles poem 5, "Don't Go," in which the speaker pleads with her *nim* not to submit to the wiles of the conquering nation. The final line of both stanzas, "This is my lover's beloved" (*nim ŭi nim*), or the "love of my lover," brings the double signification out explicitly: My *nim* (lover), also has a *nim*, who is doubly signified as myself and the nation.

51. "HYMN OF PRAISE"

The *nim* of this poem is one of the most abstract, and certainly the most heroic. "Sow the seeds of fortune in the beggars' poor soil," and "Become the bodhisattva that sprinkles tears on the heart of the weak," suggests a savior, sometimes interpreted as the Buddha himself. The "whisper of the old Paulownia" implies the music of the *kayagŭm*, the traditional twelve-string Korean harp, which was made from Paulownia wood.

52. "PLEDGING LOVE AT THE SHRINE OF NON'GAE"

Non'gae was a *kisaeng* (equivalent to a geisha) in the southern city of Chinju when it was captured by the invading forces of Japan's Hideyoshi Toyotomi in 1592. Forced to entertain the enemy men, Non'gae lured a general from a party to the Nakhwa Cliffs, where she jumped to her death in the Namgang River, pulling the general with her. Non'gae's murder-suicide is seen as an emblem of national self-sacrifice, and she is memorialized by a shrine at Ch'oksŏk Pavilion. The reference to "Chosŏn" in the fourth line is the official name of the Yi Dynasty, which ruled Korea from 1392–1910. The meaning of "Chosŏn" is usually glossed as "Land of the Morning Calm."

Manhae was not the only one in his day to make Non'gae into a poetic subject. He most likely follows the lead of Pyŏn Yŏngno's "Non'gae," which was included in the latter's 1924 collection of poems called *The Soul of Korea*:

Holy rage
Deeper than religion,
Fired passion,
Stronger than love.

Over the waves bluer, bluer than
Flowering blue-beans
Floats your spirit redder,
Redder than the poppies.

Exquisite eyebrows,
High arched in anger,
Lips like broken pomegranate
As they kissed death.

Over the waves bluer, bluer than
Flowering blue-beans
Floats your spirit redder,
Redder than the poppies.

The river lows forever,
Forever blue,
The flower of your spirit
Must be ever red.

Over the waves bluer, bluer than
Flowering blue-beans
Floats your spirit redder,
Redder than the poppies.

Pyŏn's poem adopts the stanza and refrain pattern of Western songs, particularly the Christian hymns that were disseminated among the Korean people by missionaries. As a poetic work, however, it is simple-minded, rendering Non'-gae into a "self-righteous abstraction," in the words of Solberg, whose translation I have reproduced here (202–3). In his homage, Manhae declares his devotion to Non'gae as a muse rather than as a patriot—"As a poet, I've become your lover." Non'gae is a national folk hero, but Manhae explores the more compelling topic of her treacherous heart, which calmly led a Japanese general to his death.

58. "Looking at the Moon"

This poem is created by the active metaphorical transformation of the moon into the lover's face—a transformation that is driven by the power of desire. The poet's desire for her lover leads her to endow the natural world with his attributes; to metaphorically see him in his absence. Manhae utilizes metaphor as the creative mechanism of the poem, but the Buddhist understanding that desire is the source of all phenomenal reality encourages us to look at the nature of metaphors themselves.

The lines "A year ago, I thought your face was like the moon; / Tonight the moon has become your face" are extraneous to the narrative progression of the poem. It seems to embellish the poem with an aside, first as an interjecting memory: "A year ago, I thought your face was like the moon," and then as ironic reflection on the present: "Tonight the moon has become your face." The line is more than embellishment, however. It prompts reflection upon the symmetry of reality and metaphor: Is the lover's face the original referent, and the moon the vehicle of imagination? Or is it the other way around? In the presence of one, the other is conjured, affirming both the modern literary and the Buddhist observations that all thought is ruled by the principle of metaphor.

60. "Sleep Talk"

The language of delirium in this poem echoes Tagore's *The Gardener* 42, which begins: "O mad, superbly drunk." The second stanza states,

> I have wasted my days and nights in the company of steady wise neighbours.
> Much knowing has turned my hair grey, and much watching has made my sight dim.
> For years I have gathered and heaped up scraps and fragments of things:
> Crush them and dance upon them, and scatter them all to the winds.
> For I know 'tis the height of wisdom to be drunken and go to the dogs.
>
> (RT 103–4)

Tagore embraces madness for the sake of love, seeing in madness a wisdom higher than that of common knowledge or propriety. Manhae parlays this sentiment into irrepressible sleep talk, which is another occasion to affirm his paradoxical concept of freedom: Love does not do one's bidding; love exacts its madness to which one freely submits.

As in poem 12, "Natural Virtue," the sense of the line "Love is free, virtue is fluid, marriage is a thicket of rites" contrasts the traditional rule-centered customs of courtship, chastity, and marriage with the idea that true love cannot be bound or tamed. Instead, it possesses and rules the lover.

61. "To Kyewŏrhyang"

Like Non'gae, Kyewŏrhyang was a *kisaeng* during the Hideyoshi invasions of the sixteenth century. She had a Japanese officer killed as he lay sleeping in her lap.

68. "Cuckoo"

In Chinese folk legend, the cuckoo is the spirit of King Wangdi of the ancient state of Shu. He relinquished his state to a successor, and lived to regret it. The cuckoo is thus associated with deep sorrow, particularly the sorrow of losing one's country, and it is said that it cries until blood flows from its mouth. The last line, "Better turn back, better turn back," is the semantic meaning of *pu'ryŏgi, pu'ryŏgi*, which is the onomatopoeic representation of the cuckoo's cry.

71. "Reading Tagore's Poem 'Gardenisto'"

"Gardenisto" is the Esperanto version of "gardener." Esperanto is the "universal" language invented by the Polish philologist L. L. Zamenhof (1859–1917), which is actually based on Latin and Greek root words. Esperanto had its enthusiasts in Korea, and the title of this poem indicates that Manhae had access to an Esperanto translation of Tagore.

This tribute to Tagore is inspired by Manhae's reading of *The Gardener,* Tagore's anthology of love poems, and most particularly by the eighty-fifth and final poem:

> Who are you, reader, reading my poems an hundred years hence?
> I cannot send you one simple flower from this wealth of
> the spring, one single streak of gold from yonder clouds.
> Open you doors and look abroad.
> From your blossoming garden gather fragrant memories of
> the vanished flowers of an hundred years before.
> In the joy of your heart may you feel the living joy that
> sang one spring morning, sending its glad voice across an
> hundred years.
>
> (RT 125)

In this address, Tagore compares his poetry to fragrant flowers that can be revived in the blossoming gardens of the future. Manhae's own reference to flowers and scent suggests that his reading of Tagore has, in fact, penetrated the cultural and national barriers between them. Manhae's second and third stanzas, however, are commonly read as a dispute: Tagore is taken to task for dwelling in the past instead of fighting for revolution.

It seems more logical, however, to read these lines as an argument about poetry, in continuity with the theme of the first stanza: "My friend, you weep over broken love / Your tears can't bring back scattered flowers to the bough"—the loss of *nim* creates the occasion for poetry, but one cannot enliven the present with the poetry of the past. The argument here concerns the transhistorical nature of poetry. In Manhae's own postscript, he encourages his readers to throw his poetry away like so many dried, dead flowers. Art can overcome spatial boundaries—Manhae is moved by the fragrance of Tagore's songs—but not the barrier of time. Each epoch requires its own set of actions, its own art. Although art can transport the individual across boundaries, art is still an entity within history and must progress.

73. "Love's Fire"

Suin is an emperor of Chinese legend who discovered fire. The Chinese ideographic character for *su* means torch or flint.

76. "When You Left" and
79. "Summer Nights Are Long"

The conceit of cutting out or joining together sections of time in "When You Left" harkens back to a most famous poem by Hwang Chini (1506–44), in which she folds and unfolds time:

I will break the back
of this long, midwinter night,
folding it double,
cold beneath my spring quilt
that I may draw out
the night, should my love return.

(CA 91)

Hwang Chini shortens and lengthens the night in accordance with the absence or presence of her lover. In "When You Left," Manhae simply cuts away the time of his lover's parting. "Summer Nights Are Long" plays on the prosaic observation that love's absence makes time drag, even to the point of reversing the difference in the seasonal durations of the night. "But if you come back, I'll take love's knife and cut the night into a thousand pieces" unexpectedly overturns the original conceit and draws out the night by cutting it into many pieces instead of stretching it out.

80. "Meditation"

This poem likens the mental journey of meditation to reaching a distant land by boat. In this, Manhae evokes "Peach Blossom Spring," the poem by Tao Qian (365–427) that established the dominant trope of world renunciation and harmony with nature in East Asian poetry. Tao Qian's preface tells of a fisherman of Wu-ling who rowed upstream, drawn by blossoming peach flowers, until he discovered a hidden land beyond a narrow mountain breach. There, its happy inhabitants live an abundant life off the land, free from the constraints of government. That this land cannot be found by subsequent seekers plainly signifies that it is ultimately a mental landscape, in which the true self is discovered far away from the affairs of the "world of dust." Tao Qian is often styled as the founder of Chinese nature poetry. He refused to take up office in an age of political compromise and instability, preferring the life of an impoverished farmer. In "Meditation," however, Manhae seeks to build a "heavenly land" within the world itself, thus completing the idea that heaven lies within the mind.

81. "Double Seventh"

The double seventh is the seventh day of the seventh lunar month. According to Chinese folk legend, on this day the Weaver Girl (the star Vega, in the constellation Lyra) and Herdsman (Altair, in the constellation Aquila) cross the Milky Way to consummate their love. The Weaver Girl and Herdsman met and fell in love in the days when the Silver River (the Milky Way) still touched the earth. The Weaver Girl was the granddaughter of the Queen Mother of Heaven, who was angered by the Weaver Girl's marriage to a mortal. So the Queen Mother pulled the Silver River up into the heavens, creating a barrier between the two lovers. Out of sympathy, however, she decreed that they could meet once a year, on the double seventh, when magpies soar across the river to make a bridge. These two bright stars of the autumn sky are thus folk emblems of love and separation in East Asia.

84. "Playing the Kŏmun'go"

The *kŏmun'go* is the six-stringed Korean harp, similar to the Chinese lute, known as the *qin*, and the Japanese harp, known as the *koto*.

85. "Come"

Compare this poem to *The Gardener* 12:

> If you would be busy and fill your pitcher, come, O come to my lake.
>   The water will cling round your feet and babble its secret.
>   The shadow of the coming rain is on the sands, and the clouds hang low upon the blue lines of the trees like the heavy hair above your eyebrows.
>   I know well the rhythm of your steps, they are beating in my heart.
>   Come, O come to my lake, if you must fill your pitcher.
>
> If you would be idle and sit listless and let your pitcher float on the water, come, O come to my lake.
>   The grassy slope is green, and the wild flowers beyond number.
>   Your thoughts will stray out of your dark eyes like birds from their nests.
>   Your veil will drop to your feet.
>   Come, O come to my lake, if you must sit idle.
>
> If you would leave off your play and dive in the water, come, O come to my lake.

Let your blue mantle lie on the shore; the blue water will cover you and hide you.

The waves will stand a-tiptoe to kiss your neck and whisper in your ears.

Come, O come to my lake, if you would dive in the water.

If you must be mad and leap to your death, come, O come to my lake.

It is cool and fathomlessly deep.

It is dark like a sleep that is dreamless.

There in its depths nights and days are one, and songs are silence.

Come, O come to my lake, if you would plunge to your death.

(RT 89–90)

In Tagore's poem the location is a lake rather than a garden, but they both signify the ultimate destination of death. Similar to *Gitanjali* 103, this death entails the silencing of song (see the note to poem 1, "My Lover's Silence"). In Manhae's "Come," however, death means the resolution of all opposites, including the opposition between life and death, and song and silence.

87. "Waiting"

In Buddhist cosmology, Mount Sumeru lies at the center of the universe, surrounded by the sun, moon, four continents, six pleasure heavens, and the Buddhist heaven. This is one world, which when multiplied a thousand times makes the "small thousand world." The latter is multiplied a thousand times more to make the "middle thousand world," which is finally multiplied a thousand times again to create the "large thousand world." This final vision of the universe is equivalent to the "three thousand worlds" invoked in the last stanza.

88. "The End of Love"

The poet responds to the urgent calls of her lover to come away with him before the break of dawn. Her responses suggest their immanent reunion, rendering the title, "The End of Love," consistent with this anthology's paradoxical view that love's fulfillment, in fact, lies in absence. Whereas love's silence maintains love, instantiated as the poetry of this volume, this final poem consummates love, and hence brings about the end of both love and poetry.

"Postscript: To the Reader"

This postscript has been read by some as an apology for the weakness of poetry in contrast to revolution. *Silence* was composed shortly after Manhae's three-year imprisonment by the Japanese, and for this reason some interpreters see this poetic endeavor as an underground political gesture. This reading also draws upon the last line of *Silence's* preface, "Idle Words": "I write these poems for the young lambs wandering lost on the road home from the darkening plain." Some understand this line to mean that Manhae sought to inspire young revolutionaries through the veiled words of poetry.

Manhae's direct address to his readers in this postscript is clearly inspired by the final poem of *The Gardener* (see the note for poem 71, "Reading Tagore's Poem 'Gardenisto'"). As I have read this latter poem, Manhae's argument with Tagore concerns poetry rather than revolution. Unlike Tagore, Manhae tells his readers to throw his poetry away so that they can gather the flowers of their own historical moment. As if to emphasize his own unique historical moment, the byline of this postscript dates *Silence* to the fifteenth anniversary of the Japanese annexation of Korea, as well as to his own date of birth. The annexation treaty was signed by the Korean prime minister on August 22, 1910, and on the twenty-ninth, King Sunjong issued a proclamation yielding the throne and sovereignty of his country to Japan.

Notes on the Essay

1 Manhae made his argument for clerical marriage, as well as a host of other Buddhist institutional reforms, in his *Reformation of Korean Buddhism (Chosŏn Pulgyo yusillon)*, written in 1910. The repeal of the marriage prohibition in 1926, however, was less the result of Manhae's systematic arguments, and more a sign of the degree to which Japanese Buddhism—which sanctioned monk marriage—had coopted the Korean sangha.

2 This rumor is briefly discussed in Ko Ŭn, *Han Yongun p'yongjŏn* [Critical biography of Han Yongun], 319–20.

3 This discussion appears in a 1932 article titled "Sŏn kwa insaeng" [Sŏn and life] that Manhae wrote for the magazine *Pulgyo* [Buddhism], reprinted in *Han Yongun chŏnjip* [Complete works of Han Yongun], 2:311. All primary writings referred to or quoted in this essay can be found in this six-volume collection, hereafter cited as HYC.

4 See Burton Watson, trans., *The Zen Teachings of Master Lin-chi* (New York: Columbia University Press, 1993), for a record of Linji's teachings and actions.

5 "Sŏn kwa insaeng," HYC 2:316–17.

6 Manhae turned to modern fiction in the last phase of his literary life, producing four novels between 1935 and 1939: *Hŭkp'ung* [Black Wind] (1935–36), *Huhoe* [Remorse] (1935), *Ch'orhyŏl miin* [Iron Lady] (1937), and *Pangmyŏng* [Misery] (1938–39). All four were serialized in newspapers, although *Huhoe* and *Ch'orhyŏ miin* were not completed. Manhae was a novice to the medium of fiction, and his efforts were commissioned by publishers on the basis of his national political prestige. Manhae's fiction is not successful from a literary perspective, being overly didactic and contrived in plot. Therefore, Manhae's novels have not been the subject of much

scholarship or readership. One additional fictive work, the novella *Chugŭm* [Death], was written in 1924 but never published during his lifetime.

7 "Chosŏn tongnip sŏnŏn ŭi iyu" [A rationale for the declaration of independence]," HYC 1:351.

8 The most famous instances of this theme in Korean literary history are the two *kasa* poems (long poems) by Chŏng Ch'ŏl (1537–94), "Song of Longing" and "Continued Song of Longing," written between 1585 and 1587, when he was forced into political exile from King Sŏnjo's court.

9 Manhae dates the postscript to August 29, 1925. It is interesting to note that August 29 is also his birthday. He was forty-six years old on this date, or forty-seven by Asian counting.

10 This is the reading in Kim Hyŏnsŭng, *Han'guk hyŏndaesi haesŏl* [Commentary on modern Korean poetry].

11 This is pointed out by Ch'oe Tongho, in *Han Yongun: sarang kwa hyŏkmyŏng ŭi aura* [Han Yongun: unifying love and revolution], 65–69. As one of the most recent monographs on Manhae, this text demonstrates the degree to which the political reading of *Silence* still dominates interpretation. One can note, however, that Manhae published *Siphyŏndam chuhae* [Commentary on the Ten Abstruse Discussions], a scholastic annotation of a Tang dynasty Buddhist text, in 1925—the same year *Silence* was composed. This demonstrates that revolution was not the sole preoccupation of Manhae at this time.

12 For example, in Ch'oe Namsŏn's *Paekp'al pŏnnoe* [One hundred and eight desires] (1925), and Pyŏn Yŏngno's *Chosŏn ŭi maŭm* [Heart of Korea] (1924).

13 See for example, Kim Honggyu, "Nim ŭi sojae wa chingjonghan yŏksa" [The location of *nim* and true history], 21.

14 The primary example is Song Uk's full-length commentary on *Silence* (*Nim ŭi chimmunk chŏnp'yŏn haesŏl*), which monotonously renders each poem into an allegorical discourse on the Buddhist principles of emptiness, no-mind, and enlightenment.

15 This pattern is first suggested by Paek Nakchŏng in "Simin munhakron" [Popular literature], and quite explicitly developed by Kim Chaehong in *Han Yongun munhak yŏn'gu* [The literature of Han Yongun], 99–107. Kim divides the entire corpus of *Silence* into precise subsections that correspond to these movements.

16 Burton Watson, trans., *Cold Mountain: 100 Poems by the T'ang Poet Han-shan* (New York: Columbia University Press, 1970), 57.

17 *Sijo* is the name of the regulated verse poetry that was the most popular poetic form in Korea since the fourteenth century. Like the Japanese haiku, it consists of three lines with a fixed number of syllables. The *sijo* is much longer than haiku, however, consisting of forty-five syllables (three lines of fifteen syllables), on the average, compared to the haiku's seventeen. Each *sijo* line has a pause in the middle, and therefore is usually translated and written in English as a six-line poem.

18 *Columbia Anthology of Traditional Korean Poetry,* 99; hereafter cited in the text as CA with page number.

19 "Engaged Buddhism" is a phrase that is used to designate Buddhist movements that utilize classic Buddhist teachings to address contemporary social and political problems. The phenomenon is associated primarily with Asian leaders—religious and political—who organized for peace and reform in the context of specific conflicts, such as the monk Thich Nhat Hanh during the Vietnam War. For profiles of prominent engaged Buddhists, see Christopher S. Queen and Sallie B. King, eds., *Engaged Buddhism: Buddhist Liberation Movements in Asia* (Albany: State University of New York Press, 1996).

20 "Nae ka mitnŭn Pulgyo" [My Buddhist beliefs]," HYC 2:288.

21 Ibid.

22 These statistics are cited in Pori Park, "The Modern Remaking of Korean Buddhism," 58–59.

23 "Nae ka mitnŭn Pulgyo," HYC 2:288.

24 "Sŏkka ŭi chŏngsin" [The spirit of Shakyamuni]," HYC 2:292.

25 Manhae recounts this story in "Chukta ka saranan iyagi" [From death to life]," HYC 1:251–52.

26 See note 17 for an explanation of *sijo*.

27 Sammy Edward Solberg, "The Nim-ŭi ch'immuk (Your Silence) of Han Yong-un, a Korean Poet," 201.

28 "Ch'uhwa" [Autumn flowers], HYC 1:96.

29　The custom of men writing in the persona of a woman can be dated to the Chinese poet Qu Yuan, who lived in the southern kingdom of Chu (4th–3rd c. BCE). In his long narrative poem "Encountering Sorrow," Qu fashions himself as a devoted but slandered wife who is unjustly cast out by her husband. This poem was written in protest of his treatment by the king of Chu. This precedent of using the husband-wife relationship to allegorize the minister-sovereign one partially explains why *Silence* has been read as political allegory.

30　Song Uk's 1963 essay "Manhae Han Yongun kwa R. Tago'oru" [Manhae Han Yongun and R. Tagore] provided the first comparative analysis of the two poets and established what has become a standard critique of Tagore. Song takes Tagore to task for his lack of outrage at the injustices of colonial rule and praises Manhae's superior political consciousness. More recently, Kim Chaehong reiterates the basic premises of Song's essay in *Han Yongun munhak yŏn'gu* [The literature of Han Yongun], 215–220), as does Ch'oe Tongho in *Han Yongun: sarang kwa hyŏkmyŏng ŭi aura* [Han Yongun: unifying love and revolution], 65–69.

Select Bibliography

Ch'oe Tongho. *Han Yongun: sarang kwa hyŏkmyŏng ŭi aura* [Han Yongun: unifying love and revolution]. Seoul: Kŏn'guk Taehakgyo Ch'ulp'anbu, 2001.

Das, Sisir Kumar, ed. *The English Writings of Rabindranath Tagore.* Vol. 1, *Poems.* New Delhi: Sahitya Akademi, 1994.

Evon, Gregory N. "Eroticism and Buddhism in Han Yongun's *Your Silence.*" *Korean Studies* 24 (2000): 25–52.

Han Kyejŏn. *Han Yongun ŭi nim ŭi ch'immuk* [Han Yongun's *Silence of Everything Yearned For*]. Seoul: Sŏul Taehakgyo Ch'ulp'anbu, 1996.

Han Yongun chŏnjip [Complete works of Han Yongun]. Edited by Paek Ch'ŏl et al. Seoul: Sin'gu Munhwasa, 1973.

Im Chungbin. *Manhae Han Yongun.* Seoul: Pŏmusa, 2000.

Kang, Younghill, and Francis Keely, trans. *Meditations of the Lover.* Seoul: Yonsei University Press, 1970.

Kim Chaehong. *Han Yongun munhak yŏn'gu* [The literature of Han Yongun]. Seoul: Ilchisa, 1982.

Kim Dongsung. *Selected Poems of Kim Sowŏl.* Seoul: Sung Mun'gak, 1984.

Kim Honggyu. "Nim ŭi sojae wa chingjonghan yŏksa" [The location of nim and true history]. In *Han Yongun sasang yŏngu 2.* Seoul: Minjoksa, 1981.

Kim Hyŏnsŭng. *Han'guk hyŏndaesi haesŏl* [Commentary on modern Korean poetry]. Seoul: Kwandong Publishing, 1972.

Kim, Jaihiun, and Ronald B. Hatch, trans. *Love's Silence.* Vancouver: Ronsdale Press, 1999.

Kim Sowŏl. *Chindallae-kkot* [Azaleas]. Seoul: Miraesa, 1991.

Ko Ŭn. *Han Yongun p'yongjŏn* [Critical biography of Han Yongun]. Seoul: KOREAONE Press, 2000.

Lee, Peter H., ed. *The Silence of Love: Twentieth-Century Korean Poetry.* Honolulu: University of Hawaii Press, 1980.

McCann, David R., ed. *The Columbia Anthology of Modern Korean Poetry.* New York: Columbia University Press, 2004.

Paek Nakch'ŏng. "Simin munhakron" [Popular literature]. *Ch'angjak kwa pip'yŏng* 14 (1969).

Park, Pori. "The Modern Remaking of Korean Buddhism: Korean Reform Movement during Japanese Colonial Rule and Han Yongun's Buddhism (1879–1944)." Ph.D. diss., University of California, Los Angeles, 1998.

Solberg, Sammy Edward. "The Nim-ŭi ch'immuk (Your Silence) of Han Yong-un, a Korean Poet." Ph.D. diss., University of Washington, 1971.

Song Uk. "Manhae Han Yongun kwa R. Tago'oru" [Manhae Han Yongun and R. Tagore]. *Sasanggye* 117 (1963) Reprinted in *Han Yongun sasang yŏn'gu* [The thought of Han Yongun]. Seoul: Minjoksa, 1980.

———. *Nim ŭi ch'immuk chŏnpyŏn haesŏl* [Nim ŭi ch'immuk complete commentary]. Seoul: Kwahaksa, 1974.

Sym, Myungho. *The Making of Modern Korean Poetry: Foreign Influences and Native Creativity.* Seoul: Seoul National University Press, 1982.

Yu, Beongcheon. *Han Yong-un and Yi Kwang-su: Two Pioneers of Modern Korean Literature.* Detroit: Wayne State University Press, 1992.

About the Translator

FRANCISCA CHO received her Ph.D. from the University of Chicago Divinity School and is an Associate Professor of Buddhist Studies at Georgetown University. Her publications have focused on the relationship between East Asian Buddhism and the arts, particularly literature and film.

About Wisdom

WISDOM PUBLICATIONS, a nonprofit publisher, is dedicated to preserving and transmitting important works from all the major Buddhist traditions as well as exploring related East-West themes.

To learn more about Wisdom, or to browse books online, visit our website at www.wisdompubs.org.

You may request a copy of our mail-order catalog online or by writing to:

Wisdom Publications
199 Elm Street
Somerville, Massachusetts 02144 USA
Telephone: (617) 776-7416
Fax: (617) 776-7841
Email: info@wisdompubs.org
www.wisdompubs.org

THE WISDOM TRUST

As a nonprofit publisher, Wisdom is dedicated to the publication of fine Dharma books for the benefit of all sentient beings and dependent upon the kindness and generosity of sponsors in order to do so. If you would like to make a donation to Wisdom, please do so through our Somerville office. If you would like to sponsor the publication of a book, please write or email us at the address above.

Thank you.

Wisdom is a nonprofit, charitable 501(c)(3) organization affiliated with the Foundation for the Preservation of the Mahayana Tradition (FPMT).